Perfect
Positive
Thinking

THE PERFECT SERIES

OTHER TITLES IN THE SERIES:

Perfect Positive Thinking

ALL YOU NEED
TO GET IT RIGHT
FIRST TIME

LYNN WILLIAMS

ARROW
BUSINESS BOOKS

Published by Arrow Books in 1998

3 5 7 9 10 8 6 4 2

© Lynn Williams 1998

Lynn Williams has asserted her rights under the Copyright, Designs and
Patents Act, 1988 to be identified as the author of this work

First published by
Arrow Books Limited
20 Vauxhall Bridge Road, London SW1V 2SA

Random House Australia (Pty) Limited
20 Alfred Street, Milsons Point
Sydney, New South Wales 2061, Australia

Random House New Zealand Limited
18 Poland Road, Glenfield
Auckland 10, New Zealand

Random House South Africa (Pty) Limited
Endulini, 5a Jubilee Road, Parktown 2193, South Africa

Papers used by Random House UK Limited are natural, recyclable
products made from wood grown in sustainable forests. The
manufacturing processes conform to the environmental regulations
of the country of origin

Companies, institutions and other organizations wishing to make bulk
purchases of any business books published by Random House should
contact their local bookstore or Random House direct:
Special Sales Director
Random House
20 Vauxhall Bridge Road
London SW1V 2SA
Tel: 0171 840 8470 Fax: 0171 828 6681

Random House UK Limited Reg. No. 954009
ISBN 0 09 926937 6

Set in Bembo by
SX Composing DTP, Rayleigh, Essex
Printed and bound in Great Britain by
Cox & Wyman Ltd, Reading, Berkshire

British Cataloguing in Publication Data
A catalogue record for this book is available from the British Library

CONTENTS

INTRODUCTION

PERFECT POSITIVE THINKING

Some people are natural positive thinkers. They seem to have discovered the secrets of:

- optimism
- independence
- flexibility
- enthusiasm
- enjoyment

They always bounce back no matter what's thrown at them, and they nearly always seem to be able to:

- set productive goals for themselves
- face challenges confidently
- persevere in difficult circumstances
- continue to grow and develop
- work through problems
- be self-motivated and self-reliant
- co-operate interactively with others and enjoy relationships
- work and play creatively, productively and effectively
- help and encourage others

This book looks at how positive thinking can be achieved, and considers ways of overcoming the negative thoughts and feelings that often get in the way.

The aim is to provide a practical manual for anyone wishing to develop the skills of positive thinking, and it is set out in two parts:

- **Part One** covers the positive things that people who are natural positive thinkers already do. It specifically examines the skills, priorities, attitudes and techniques they employ that foster and encourage positive attitudes and productive thinking, such as:

- Sense of purpose
- Optimism
- Energy – physical, mental and emotional well-being
- Motivation
- Realism – practical planning rather than wishful thinking

Each of these 'life skills' is the subject of a separate chapter looking at what it is, its benefit to positive thinking, and suggesting ways in which it might be developed.

- **Part Two** looks at the problems that get in the way of developing a positive approach to life. These include:
  - Negativity
  - Indecision
  - The comfort zone
  - Hurry sickness
  - Demand Thinking
  - Comparisons

Each problem is the subject of a separate chapter acknowledging that the problem exists; explaining why; and suggesting ways of overcoming it.

WHAT IS POSITIVE THINKING?

Most of us know at least one person we would consider to be a positive thinker, someone who is, on the whole:

- constructive rather than destructive
- up-beat rather than gloomy
- friendly rather than hostile
- encouraging rather than obstructive
- enthusiastic rather than disheartening
- positive rather than negative

They can be relied upon to think and act positively even when life is hard for them, and despite hardships and set-backs, they continue to lead satisfying, happy, useful lives.

Lucky them.

So is positive thinking inborn, genetic – a naturally sunny attitude to life? Or is it something that we can all learn to develop?

The answer to both questions is, paradoxically, yes.

Most young children appear to be natural positive thinkers. They are often profoundly optimistic, and their belief in themselves and their abilities is unquenchable, even in the face of discouragement. They seem unimpressed by negative feedback and failure, and are less affected by negative beliefs about themselves than adults are.

This robustness may well be inborn – it would certainly be an advantage for young children to be relatively immune to discouragement, with all the trial-and-error learning they have to go through in the course of growing up.

However, by adolescence most of us have succumbed to a degree of negative thinking, and sufficient pessimism to protect ourselves against failure and disappointment.

Positive thinkers, though, are affected less than most. Although they add a hearty dose of realism to the extreme insouciance of childhood, they still retain several valuable childlike qualities:

- They tend to disregard failure unless, or until, it is recurrent and unavoidable
- They ignore comparisons with others and prefer to evaluate themselves on their own terms
- They place a higher value on effort and commitment than on ability as a measure of self-worth
- They pay little attention to negative occurrences – rather than going over them again and again, they let them fade from their memories quickly and naturally

As a consequence, it is nearly as hard to de-motivate positive thinkers as it is young children, with the result that they are happier and often more productive than the general run of adults.

If it's true that we learn how to be negative pessimists (having been positive optimists as children), it's fair to assume that we can un-learn our acquired negativity by copying the attitudes of natural positive thinkers.

What can we learn from them?

Positive thinkers give much more of their time and attention to what is positive than to what is negative. However, they don't just look on the bright side, they take positive steps to ensure that there is ample bright side for them to look upon. Positive thinkers don't just think positive, they act positively too. They behave in ways that actively foster a confident approach to life:

- They have a strong sense of purpose
- They think in optimistic ways
- They foster energy and resilience to stress
- They are strongly self-motivated
- They are realists

The first part of this book looks at ways of developing these same positive attributes; while the second part looks at what is likely to get in the way of them.

Part One:
POSITIVE ATTITUDES

This section considers the beliefs, attitudes and behaviours that characterize natural positive thinkers, and looks at practical ways of developing them:

1. **Sense of purpose**
2. **Optimism**
3. **Energy**
4. **Motivation**
5. **Realism**

SENSE OF PURPOSE

WHAT IS A SENSE OF PURPOSE?

Many positive thinkers have an overall aim or direction in life – a sense of purpose.

For people who are naturally positive, it's this sense of purpose that gives order and meaning to their lives. They live with intention, moving purposefully towards desired outcomes and objectives rather than drifting aimlessly, carried along by the eddies and currents of circumstance.

People with purpose seem to be able to work more patiently and productively in pursuit of their aims, and will often work co-operatively with others to accomplish mutual goals.

They feel in control of their lives. They know what's important to them and set out to accomplish it. Because they have a clear idea of what they are aiming for, they're often willing to take well-calculated risks in order to achieve it. They're also willing to learn new skills, to experiment, and they are able to approach problems and hurdles creatively.

People with a sense of purpose can:	*People without a sense of purpose may:*
make long-term plans	have to make stop-gap provisions
retain a sense of balance	become driven, obsessive or apathetic
focus on what's important to them	get bogged down in trivia
get their wants and preferences met	find their needs sidelined
have an overview of their direction	go round in circles and come to dead-ends
know when they've reached their targets	be unsure of what they've achieved
take their values and priorities into account	find others setting the agenda
continually develop their skills and talents	get into a rut
always have somewhere to direct their energies	become frustrated

WHY IS A SENSE OF PURPOSE IMPORTANT?

It's very easy to develop a negative attitude when you continually have to make stop-gap provisions, get bogged down in trivia, feel frustrated and in a rut, and when you suspect that you're going round in circles and reaching dead-ends while others are setting the agenda and sidelining your needs.

On the other hand, retaining a positive outlook is relatively simple when you can focus on what's important to you, direct your energy into developing your skills and talents, know your wants and preferences will be met, and can make long-term plans that take your values and priorities into account.

The value of purpose

There is a great deal of confidence and certainty to be gained from knowing what you want to do and why. When you have a strong, clear overview of your direction, you can relate your actions to an end purpose rather than just undertaking a series of meaningless tasks. You are consequently much more likely to stay motivated and on top of things, and retain a sense of movement and momentum rather than becoming frustrated and stagnating.

You're also much more likely to make effective plans and decisions when you are in pursuit of clear aims. With a definite sense of where you want to go, you can be flexible and creative about how you get there. There's usually more than one route to any objective even when there are setbacks, and you often have several options about how to accomplish a specific purpose. Knowing clearly what you are aiming for allows you to recognize and make use of any opportunities that come your way.

A sense of purpose further fosters a positive outlook by:
- encouraging whole-heartedness rather than half-heartedness
- inviting you to do the things you really *want* to do rather than the things you *should* do, or that other people think you *ought* to do
- developing your individual identity and self-expression

through following your own ideas
- encouraging a deeper, wider understanding of yourself and your place in the scheme of things

Unfortunately, we can get so caught up in the minutiae of everyday life that the overall picture gets lost. We reach the end of the day, week, or even a year feeling that although we've been so busy we've hardly paused for breath, we've still not actually achieved anything. So, in practical terms, having a sense of purpose gives an overview of the situation that makes it easier to:
- know where to put time, talents and effort
- make decisions
- set and achieve goals and targets
- plan effective action
- know when to say no
- prioritize conflicting demands
- weigh up the pros and cons of actions and decisions
- recognize and use opportunities
- evaluate consequences and commitments
- be proactive and take the initiative
- take calculated risks – and calculate the risk in the first place
- have control over your life
- plan a timetable, balance activities and arrange your time effectively
- know what you want to achieve, and recognize when you've achieved it

DEVELOPING A SENSE OF PURPOSE

Having a sense of purpose is one of the major keys to developing a positive outlook on life. Developing a sense of purpose or direction means knowing:
- who you are
- where you want to go
- why you want to go there

To do this you need to assess your:
- values and ideals

- roles in life
- purpose in life

And you need to be able to:
- set goals
- draw up action plans
- establish your priorities

Your values and ideals
Knowing what is important to you is a crucial first step in deciding your direction in life.

Different things are significant to different people. One person may place a very high value on solitude and time alone, another may feel this is much less important than time spent with friends. One person may value security highly, while another values freedom even at the expense of safety. Each individual has a different set of values and prioritizes them differently.

What is important to you? Values that other people have often found meaningful include:

freedom	trust	family
security	variety	career
comfort	integrity	friends
honesty	creativity	simplicity
adventure	education	truthfulness
being needed	intelligence	achievement
independence	peace of mind	spiritual values
animal welfare	nature and environment	political activity

List your own values
Think about the values you hold and write them down. When you make your list consider what is important to you and what ideals you hold. You may find it helpful to ask yourself:
- What am I proud of about myself?
- Which values have meaning for me?
- What do I value in others and want to develop in myself?

- Which values do I want to stand for and be associated with in the world?

Example:

My values:

I am proud of my:	The values with meaning for me are:
honesty	career
creativity	variety
intelligence	integrity
cheerfulness	self-expression

The things I value in others and want to develop are:	The values I want to be associated with are:
patience	education
tolerance	simplicity
commitment to friends	making a difference

These are where your strongest drives and most compelling motivations are to be found. A life lived with due consideration of your values and ideals is bound to be more positive than one that ignores or marginalizes them.

The person in the above example may wonder, for instance, if getting married and having a family 'ought' to be a higher priority than their career or commitment to friends. Or they may wonder if self-expression is an indulgence deserving little time and attention. One glance at their list of values, however, makes it clear that ignoring these things would probably leave them feeling unfulfilled and unhappy in a life that had little meaning for them.

Your roles

Once you've clarified your values, think about the roles you are asked to play in your life.

There are four main areas into which most roles fall:
- career and work
- home and family
- social and community
- personal and spiritual

PERFECT POSITIVE THINKING

Some people's roles fall largely into one or maybe two main areas, others are spread evenly across the board. Some people have many roles, while others focus on fewer. Some people like to concentrate their attention on one area, others prefer a wider balance. Some people play similar roles in different areas (being a carer, for example, both within the family and in a professional capacity), others have widely differing roles.

Some familiar roles include:

Career and Work:

teacher	mentor	salesperson
artist	leader	service provider
manager	ideas-person	designer
team-member	ambassador	key-holder

Home and Family:

carer	cook	home-maker
friend	partner	gardener
parent	teacher	dog owner
grandparent	nurturer	entertainer
brother/sister	protector	house owner
son/daughter	comforter	

Social and Community:

friend	sick visitor	car owner
neighbour	charity fund-raiser	local resident
guide-leader	community activist	environmental worker

Personal and Spiritual:

artist	student	catalyst
hiker	meditator	peacemaker
adventurer	personal trainer	self-nurturer

Think about your roles, and think about what you actually *do* in each of them. You may, for example, be employed as a secretary or sales manager. Your roles within that job could include mentor, motivator, administrator, team worker, whatever. You may be a parent, but within that role you could choose to be anything from a protector to a nutritionist, to a coach, to a playgroup leader, to a companion. Within the same role, some people see themselves as an enabler, others as a comforter. It depends on individual values and choices.

List your roles

Be as detailed or as broad in your definition of roles as you wish. Some areas of your life may break down into several highly specific roles. For others, you may decide that several functions can be grouped together into one encompassing role. It is entirely up to you what you consider a separate, clearly-defined and easily recognizable role.

When surveying your roles, you may find it helps to consider:
- your responsibilities
- the positions you hold
- the roles you are required to play in each of these positions
- your responsibilities to yourself
- your leisure-time and personal roles

Example:
My roles:

Work:
salesperson
manager
display/merchandiser
trainer

Home:
home-maker
cook
friend
partner

Community:
treasurer of Sales Association
member of Women In Business
local skittles team member

Personal:
own fitness trainer
own relaxation consultant

Do your roles reflect your values?

When you have decided what your roles are, it can sometimes be quite revealing to cross-match them against your values:

Example:

	honesty	creativity	caring	trust	solitude	family	variety
friend	✓		✓	✓			
housewife			✓			✓	
supporter			✓	✓			
mother	✓		✓	✓		✓	
secretary							
telephone canvasser							

In the above example there is a very poor match between roles and values. Valued things such as creativity, solitude and variety are being neglected, while the roles of secretary and telephone canvasser fulfil none of the values expressed (though they might have been taken on to provide variety and then proved disappointing).

The above is an extreme example, but we *are* sometimes called upon to fulfil roles that in no way reflect our values and ideals.

Likewise, we sometimes have values that are unexpressed in our daily roles.

When this happens we need to either bring our values into our roles, or adjust our roles to fit our values. To express their creativity, the person in the example above could, for instance:

- find a more creative job, even if this meant cutting back on other roles
- be more actively creative in their role of housewife and/or mother
- make time for creative pursuits by dropping the roles of secretary and canvasser
- explore the possibility of a more creative role in their current secretarial job (desk-top publishing, leaflet design, press-release writing, etc.)

Positive thinkers can be quite determined about matching their roles and values. When a role doesn't express their values they change it, negotiate it, or as a last resort even dump it!

Your purpose in life

Knowing what your values and your roles are, and having considered how the two complement each other, you are now in a good position to think about your purpose in life.

Being able to summarize succinctly who you are and what your purpose is gives you a useful rule of thumb to make choices and gauge decisions by. It helps to prevent drifting and side-tracking without being either rigid or repressive.

Look over your values and roles and see what suggests itself.

Values:	Roles:	Purpose in life:
simplicity	analyst	To bring order out of chaos!
integrity	scientist	
truthfulness	home-maker	
making a difference	organizer	
order	gardener	

Your purpose in life is a deeply personal assertion. It clarifies for you (and you alone) what you feel you are *about*. It can be anything from one line to one page long, but it should be:
• personal
• positive
• an accurate reflection of your values

Aim for something that looks, feels and sounds right to you, then write it down and put it somewhere where you will see it often.

Example 1:
To nurture the pathways of self-expression for myself and for others; to be sensitive to and foster creativity in all its forms; to encourage and make freely available the means of self-expression in others; to believe in the creative potential of all places, at all times, and in all people.

Arts Administrator, Tutor and Mother

Example 2:
To boldly go where no one has gone before – and bring back photographs.

Photographer and Explorer

Example 3:
To maintain the highest standards of self-respect, and to actively ensure that every individual within my circle of influence is treated with thoughtfulness, dignity and consideration.

Disability Activist, Carer

When you know what your life purpose is, you can plan the things you need to do in order to carry it out. You can plan activities and set goals for yourself, knowing that they reflect your values and ideals. This purposefulness is at the root of the confidence and self-assurance natural to positive thinkers.

Setting goals and planning your actions

Goals are the things you want to do, the things you intend to achieve. Once you know what is important to you, you can define your goals much more clearly and accurately.

Look at your values and your purpose in life, and think about what you want to achieve. Imagine how you might achieve your purpose through one or more of your life roles.

Example:

Purpose (part):	. . . to encourage, empower and develop those around me . . .
Values:	Independence, empowerment
Role:	Mentor
Goal:	Increase Alistair's confidence and organizational skills
Idea:	Delegate organizing seminar to Alistair
Purpose (part):	. . . to build bridges and find out what we have in common . . .
Values:	Honesty, openness, commitment
Role:	Friend
Goal:	Get closer to Paula
Idea:	Arrange to meet for coffee and chat

Once you have an idea of what your goals are, you can begin to define them more clearly so that you can plan your actions.

Smarts
Make sure your goals are clear, well thought out and well defined. They need to be:

Specific   Keep goals simple and direct. If a goal seems complicated, break it down into two or three simpler ones.

Measurable   Include some way of assessing your progress, and of knowing when you have reached your goal.

Achievable   Be realistic, don't aim for something you have little faith in achieving. If you reach this goal, you can always set yourself another, more challenging one afterwards.

Result-based What do you want to achieve? For example: 'Eat five helpings of fruit a day' is an action (which we'll come to shortly). It isn't a goal because it doesn't say why you're doing it. Your actual goal might be: 'Improve my resistance to disease' or 'Improve my health'.

Time-tabled Have some idea of how long you expect your goal to take, and when you want to achieve it by. This will give you a framework when you come to plan your actions.

Supported   Decide what support you could use – who could help, how and when.

Plan your actions
Next, consider the practical steps needed to achieve your purpose. For each of your goals, think about the actions you will have to take to accomplish it. If your goal seems

complicated or a long way off, break it down into smaller steps, or targets, to make planning easier.

Example:

Purpose (part):	. . . to encourage, empower and develop those around me . . .
Values:	Independence, empowerment
Role:	Mentor
Goal:	Increase Alistair's confidence and organizational skills
Idea:	Delegate organizing seminar to Alistair
Actions:	Arrange meeting between Alistair and Jan Gordon by 1st May
	Review aims and objectives of seminar with Alistair at Monday meeting
	Update and hand over seminar file at Monday meeting
	Brief Sue on plan (tomorrow)
	Ensure contact and address books are up-to-date and available
	Schedule twice-weekly meetings with Alistair to review progress

Long-term Planning

Long-term planning is no different from short-term planning, it just requires more steps. Be bold and positive when choosing your long-term goals – decide on your goal *then* think about how to get there, don't let current circumstances limit your dreams.

There are two keys to successful long-term planning:
• When you have long-term goals, plan a series of targets between where you are now and where you want to be. This gives you a series of short steps, rather than one big intimidating jump, between you and your goal.
• Instead of working forward from your current position, *work back* from your ultimate goal to where you are now.

Example:

I am here		I want to get here
Totally unfit		Run a marathon

Start   **End Goal**

Where would you need to be, what would you need to be *already* doing, to make your ultimate goal likely?

Totally unfit		Able to run ten miles relatively comfortably	Run a marathon
		Target	**End Goal**

This is one of your targets.

Now, what would you need to be doing already to make this target of running ten miles achievable?

Totally unfit	Jogging five miles three times a week	Able to run ten miles relatively comfortably	Run a marathon
Start	**Target 1**	**Target 2**	**End Goal**

Keep asking the question until you arrive back at where you are now. The secret is to keep breaking your targets down into smaller and smaller stages until you arrive at steps that you firmly believe you can achieve:

Values:	Health and strength
Goal:	Run a marathon
Target 1:	Jogging five miles three times a week
Mini-Targets:	1. Walk twenty minutes three times a week by end of June
	2. Mixed walking and jogging twenty minutes by mid-August
	3. Jogging twenty minutes by end of September
	4. Increase distance by x amount each week until Target 1 achieved
Actions:	Get proper footwear
	Check targets and timetable with fitness centre
	Plan route
	Health check with GP
	Find suitable warm-up exercises

PERFECT POSITIVE THINKING

Prioritizing

Knowing what to do is essential. Knowing what *not* to do is quite useful too.

When you are clear what your life purpose is, prioritizing demands and tasks becomes much more simple:

- Does this contribute to my purpose in life?
- If yes, then do it
- If no, then don't do it

If you're still undecided, or you're not sure if what's come up is a genuine opportunity or just a side-track, consider your values and roles:

Think of your roles and values as a grid

	one of my values	*not* one of my values
one of my roles	Quadrant 1	Quadrant 3
not one of my roles	Quadrant 2	Quadrant 4

Quadrant 1 is the most important. Anything that reflects both your values and your role in life is clearly a high priority and should get the lion's share of your time and attention.

Quadrant 2 is the next most important. Something that relates to your values, even if it isn't currently one of your roles, should be thought about. Even if you can't take on the appropriate role yourself, could you delegate it to somebody who can?

Quadrant 3 is less important. It may be a task that falls within your role, but if it's not in line with your values, dispatch it efficiently, then look at how it's arisen and see if there's something you can do to stop it coming up again.

Quadrant 4 tasks and demands are your lowest priority, reflecting neither your values nor any of your roles. Keep them to a minimum and dispatch them speedily. If tasks in this quadrant keep growing, you may need to plan a major lifestyle shake-up.

PUTTING IT ALL TOGETHER

Take some time to think about and plan your direction. It's worth actually writing down your aims and objectives to clarify your mind, and also to put them 'out there' rather than just keeping them in your own head. Keep a notebook or loose-leaf folder and use a fresh page for each of the following headings:

* My purpose in life
* My goals for the next five years
* My goals for this year
* My goals for the coming three months
* My main priority this week
* Today's priorities

Review and update your objectives regularly, and remember to congratulate yourself when you stick to a priority and/or achieve a goal.

SUMMARY

Positive thinkers have a sense of purpose.

Enhance your natural sense of purpose:
* Decide your purpose in life
  * understand what your values are
  * understand what roles you play
  * make sure your roles reflect your values
  * make a personal, positive declaration stating your life's purpose
* Set goals to achieve your purpose in life
* Plan actions to achieve your goals
* Prioritize your activities

2

OPTIMISM

WHAT IS OPTIMISM?

Optimism is the ability to see the positive side of things rather than the negative.

Optimistic thinkers are usually positive people because they approach life with the expectation that a happy outcome is both desirable and possible. Optimists are sometimes mistakenly accused of wearing rose-tinted spectacles – of believing that everything will turn out for the best in the end, so why worry? True optimism, however, doesn't just mean turning a blind eye to problems, it means actively searching out the positive factors in the situation.

Optimists anticipate success and look for evidence of it. Pessimists, on the other hand, anticipate failure and look for evidence of *that*. Consequently, when things go wrong – and even optimists will admit that things go wrong occasionally – pessimists will say 'there you are, what did I say? I'm a real failure.' Optimists, on the other hand, will indignantly look for the reasons *why* it went wrong, and do things differently in the future as a result.

Optimists are often:	Pessimists tend to be:
confident, adventurous and willing to take chances	anxious, apprehensive and timid
open, outgoing, approving of others and broadminded	defensive, critical, suspicious and withdrawn
energetic, productive and positive	passive, dependent and negative
enthusiastic, vibrant, light-hearted and relaxed	alarmist, gloomy, despondent and tense
in control and buoyant	fatalistic and fearful

WHY IS OPTIMISM USEFUL?

Seeing the positive aspects of difficult or disappointing circumstances gives optimists the courage and ability to carry on and try again. They can learn from mistakes and apply that knowledge to subsequent events, rather than either avoiding similar situations in future, or fatalistically repeating the same errors.

Optimists look at their lives in terms of success rather than set-backs. They focus on what they have achieved, however little, rather than dwelling on what might have been and where they have failed. They also have a much broader definition of success than pessimists, taking any sign of progress as evidence of achievement.

This means that optimists are able to:
- maintain a healthy self-esteem – they 'fail' less often
- be more flexible and creative in the face of set-backs
- deal with problems rather than avoiding them
- explore opportunities more thoroughly and extensively
- follow their own direction – they need less reassurance
- take greater, and better calculated, risks
- maintain higher expectations of themselves and others
- maintain their energy and motivation
- enjoy their own and others' achievements

DEVELOPING OPTIMISM

Some people may be born optimists, but for those of us who aren't, it is still possible to achieve a much more optimistic outlook on life.

Psychologists looking into optimism found that optimists shared many of the same attitudes to success and failure, and that these were very different from the attitudes of pessimists.

In particular they found that optimists believe that:

Success is:	Failure is:
Permanent – once a success, always a success	*Temporary* – it's just this time and won't last
Individual and inner-directed – success is a result of personal character and effort	*Due to outside factors* independent of the individual
Generalized – success in one thing means success is possible in all things	*Specific* – just because one thing fails it doesn't mean that others will

Interestingly, they found that *pessimists* believe exactly the opposite. They assume that:

Failure is:	**Success is:**
Permanent – once a failure, always a failure	*Temporary* – it's just this time and won't last
Individual and inner-directed – failure is a result of personal characteristics	*Due to outside factors* independent of the individual
Generalized – failure in one thing means failure is inevitable in all things	*Specific* – just because one thing succeeds it doesn't mean that anything else will

You can increase your positive thinking by deliberately adopting the optimists' way of looking at things. Doing this consciously and persistently, you can gradually change your habits of thinking and achieve a more optimistic and positive frame of mind.

You need to:
- focus on your successes – acknowledge and enjoy them
- minimize your failures – put them into perspective

Focus on your successes

Consciously search out and notice success and pleasure in your life. Change any negative thoughts that accompany success or enjoyment into positive ones. Remember that optimists firmly believe that:

Success is permanent: replace any ideas that success won't last with a positive appreciation of its permanency:

Negative thought	**Positive thought**
I was lucky that time	I usually succeed
It was just a fluke, it won't last	I've done it once, I can do it again
I'm having a good time for once	I usually enjoy myself
I made a good impression, but it won't last	I've made a good beginning, I can build on it

Success is individual and inner-directed: substitute any negative thoughts about it being just a lucky chance with ones that acknowledge your skill and effort:

Negative thought	Positive thought
It was just luck	I planned well and was prepared
I was lucky that time	I worked hard for it and I deserve it
It was a lucky chance	I saw the opportunity and seized it
It was the rest of the team that won	I played an important part in our success

Success is general: When you succeed in one thing, remind yourself that you will succeed in other things too:

Specific thought	Positive thought
James likes me	I'm a likeable person
That was easy	I'm good at this
That meeting was okay	I'm effective in meetings
I managed to do that bit	I'll be able to do the rest of it now

Minimize your failures

Consciously put your failures and disappointments into perspective against a positive background. Optimists always remind themselves that:

Failure is temporary: replace catastrophic *always* and *never* thoughts with more positive ones:

Negative thought	Positive thought
I always get it wrong	I made a mistake this time
I'm always going to be stuck here	I'm here for the time being
It happens every time	It happened this time
I've never been happy	I'm unhappy at the moment

Failure is due to outside factors: stop blaming yourself and consider all the other reasons why you might have failed:

Negative thought	Positive thought
I'm stupid, I don't understand this	I don't have enough information
I'm slow and incompetent	I don't have the right equipment
I'm no good at making decisions	I don't have the right advice yet
Everything's my fault	There are a number of reasons why we failed

Failure is specific: substitute positive thoughts for any generalized *nobody, nothing, never* ones you may have:

Negative thought	Positive thought
Nobody likes me	It's not easy getting to know people here
I'm stupid	I'm not familiar with this particular subject
Nothing ever works	This particular thing didn't work
Life is hard	This specific problem is a challenge

Optimists also have other useful approaches to life that you can copy. They:
- look for positive features rather than negative ones
- focus on solutions rather than problems
- adopt broadminded attitudes and support positive explanations
- act on the most generous interpretation of events

Look for positive features
When you're confronted with a negative situation – a disagreement, for example, a disappointing result, or something that hasn't quite worked out – actively and consciously look for the positive elements before wading into the negative criticism.

Adopt the **PIN** code and evaluate the situation in the following order:

P – first look for something **positive** about it

I – next look for something **interesting** about it

N – only when you've done that, look for anything **negative** about it

Examples:
Situation: a diet that didn't work out:

Positive	I had the will-power to keep to it for one week
	I lost one pound
	I started to feel more energetic

Interesting	I discovered some new low-fat recipes
	I learned more about a healthy diet
	I found out where the local swimming-pool was

| **Negative** | I went back to my old habits after a week |

Situation: an unavoidable move to a new area:

Positive	Opportunity to explore new places
	Chance to make new friends
	Opportunity to leave old habits behind

Interesting   Chance to see how I cope with change
              Chance to think about what I want for the
              future

Negative   Saying goodbye to old friends
              Leaving the safe and familiar

Focus on solutions

When you know what the negative aspects are – having
already found out the positive and the interesting ones –
don't just dwell on them, work out what went wrong and
decide how you will do things differently in the future.
Look for solutions.

Examples:
Situation: a diet that didn't work out:

Negative situation	Possible solutions
I went back to my old eating habits after a week	Recognize 'danger zones' and plan accordingly
	Team up with a friend for support
	Plan plenty of activities
	Plan and buy two weeks' food at start
	Remember never to shop when hungry
	Plan fitness-related activity to boost metabolism in second week

Situation: an unavoidable move to a new area:

Negative situation	Possible solutions
Saying goodbye to old friends	Write regularly
	Plan a get-together at halfway point
	Invite individuals to stay regularly
	Start 'round-robin' tape between us all
Leaving the safe and familiar	Find out about new area before moving
	Visit for the day
	Write to local branch of professional society
	Remember that everywhere becomes familiar after a while

Adopt broadminded attitudes

There are usually several ways to interpret situations, particularly when it comes to other people's behaviour.
Optimists generally adopt the most broadminded and

favourable ones, and give people the benefit of the doubt wherever possible.

Before automatically deciding what something 'means', think consciously about the other possible interpretations.

Examples:

A friend is irritable and brusque:

Negative interpretation	**Positive interpretation**
She doesn't like me any more	She's worried about something

My partner is feeling tired and run down

Negative interpretation	**Positive interpretation**
He must be ill or sickening for something	He's been very busy recently

An employer is unusually critical:

Negative interpretation	**Positive interpretation**
They're looking for reasons to sack me	They're under pressure too

Act on the most generous interpretation

Unless, or until, they have evidence to the contrary, optimists act as if their most benign interpretation of the situation was the true one.

Follow their lead and consider how you can act positively.

Examples:

A friend is irritable and brusque:

Positive interpretation	**Beneficial action**
She's worried about something	I'll stay friendly towards her and make sure there's an opportunity to talk if she wants to

My partner is feeling tired and run down:

Positive interpretation	**Beneficial action**
He's been very busy recently	We'll take this weekend off to relax and I'll take responsibility for some of his chores

An employer is unusually critical:

Positive interpretation	Beneficial action
They're under pressure too	I'll be extra diligent and pleasant at work to take some of the stress off

SUMMARY

Positive thinkers have optimism.

Enhance your natural optimism:
- Focus on pleasure and success
  - success is permanent
  - success is due to your own individual talent and hard work
  - success is general
- Minimize your failures
  - failure is temporary
  - failure is due to outside factors
  - failure is specific
- Look for all the positive things first
- Focus on solutions
- Adopt broadminded attitudes
- Act on the most generous interpretation of events

3
ENERGY

WHAT IS ENERGY?

Energy is that liveliness and vigour with which some people approach their activities. It's both the physical expression and a fundamental component of the enthusiasm they seem to infuse into everyday life.

Energy has two major aspects:
- **zest** – the get-up-and-go that initiates activity
- **stamina** – the resilience that allows activity to continue

Energy that has both these components confers a high degree of indefatigability and buoyancy on the lucky recipient, making them not only lively and active with a relish for life, but resistant to stress and illness and able to bounce back from knocks and set-backs.

WHY IS ENERGY USEFUL?

People who are positive frequently have a high degree of physical robustness and resilience. To some extent this may be the result of their positive attitude, rather than the cause of it. However, there's no denying that you need energy and resilience to do the things you want to do and to maintain a positive outlook on life. Constant tiredness and aches and pains, or feelings of being 'out-of-sorts' and 'below par' limit your activities and significantly reduce your quality of life.

A sense of purpose and an optimistic outlook are, in themselves, great energizers. Energy needs a firm physical platform as well, though. The physical capacity, as well as the mental and emotional ability, to get through the day with direction, determination and spirit depends on fostering the optimum conditions for health and fitness, and treating your body with tolerance and respect.

Although we may not be able to completely avoid illness, accidents and old age – human life unfortunately just isn't like that – we can take care of our physical health in such a way as to achieve the maximum sense of well-being whatever our circumstances.

DEVELOPING ENERGY

There are few magic potions or miracle cures. Developing energy and vitality depends on the ordinary, everyday principles of good nutrition, adequate exercise and sufficient rest. Adopting simple good habits in these areas can, however, bring about a seemingly miraculous improvement, especially if your body has been used to running on empty.

Instant lifts

Beware of some things that seem to promise an instant energy boost:

- Tea and coffee – a strong cup of coffee or tea is still one of the most popular pick-me-ups. One cup is fine, but beware of using it to compensate for more serious energy depletion
- Sugar – a sugary snack can lower blood-sugar levels which will, paradoxically, leave you feeling tired and depressed after a brief buzz
- Alcohol – it will do little to actually raise your energy and can cause a deterioration in performance

If you need a quick burst of refreshment try:

- Fresh air – a few deep breaths of fresh air outside or at an open window will wake you up and keep you going
- Starch – better than sugar for providing energy, starchy foods release their sugars over a longer period without swamping your system. Wholemeal bread, cereals, bananas and dried fruit are all good energy providers
- Music – put on some fast, up-beat music for extra pep. If you find yourself singing or tapping your feet, even better.

Stress

The biggest threat to energy is stress. A little of it can add a
bit of spice to life; too much is a major problem. Try these
suggestions for keeping it under control:

- **Take time to relax** – just five minutes, morning and
  evening, spent consciously calming down and letting go
  of tension can make an enormous difference
- **Get to the root of the problem** – find out what's
  causing the stress and plan positive action to overcome it
- **Get support** – talk over what's making you stressed
  with someone you trust. Just putting it into words often
  helps to put things into perspective and makes them
  easier to deal with
- **Work off tension** – regular exercise not only helps
  release frustration and tension in the short term, it also
  helps to strengthen the body against the long-term
  effects of stress
- **Be assertive** – don't say 'yes' or 'maybe' when you
  mean 'no'. Don't put up with people treating you badly,
  tell them politely but firmly to stop. Nothing is worth
  putting up with if it makes you ill
- **Laugh more** – strange but true: even a false smile and
  false laughter have a relaxing and enlivening effect on the
  body
- **Take a deep breath** – when stressed, breathing tends
  to be rapid, shallow and high up in the chest. To relax,
  breathe slowly and deeply, using all of your chest right
  down to your stomach
- **Look after yourself** – don't put extra stress on your
  body by asking it to cope with a poor diet, too much
  alcohol, or too many cigarettes
- **Take breaks** – it sounds obvious, but don't forget to
  take breaks at regular intervals. Things can seem so
  urgent and important that holidays, rest and enjoyment
  drop right to the bottom of the list as 'non-essentials'
- **Accept that stress is a part of life** – however nice it
  would be, the time will probably never come when life
  is completely free from stress or worry. Knowing that

you can meet the challenge and deal with stress is more positive than living in fear of it

Optimum energy

To make the most of your physical health, and maintain and increase your well-being:

- Eat a balanced diet
- Exercise regularly
- Remember the three Rs:
  - rest
  - relaxation
  - recreation

These factors are to some extent interdependent. You will, for example, sleep better when you take regular exercise. If, however, you have any doubts about your health, or are uncertain about the wisdom of changing your diet or starting to exercise, then see your GP who will be able to advise you accordingly.

Eat a balanced diet

Just a few very simple changes can turn the average diet into a healthy eating plan:

Increase:

- **Fibre** – choose complex carbohydrates such as wholemeal bread, pasta, oats, brown rice, beans and the humble potato more often
- **Vitamins** – rather than taking supplements, get more vitamins from fresh fruit and vegetables to protect against heart disease and cancer. Five portions a day is recommended
- **Low-fat protein** – opt for chicken, offal and fish more often, grilled or baked, not fried

Decrease:

- **Fat** – make use of the low-fat alternatives to butter and margarine. Replace milk, yoghurt, and cheese with low-

fat and semi-skimmed varieties. Cut back on fried food. Save cream, crisps, and chocolate for special occasions
* **Sugar** – gradually reduce the amount you add to tea, coffee and cereals. Watch out for added sugar in prepared foods
* **Tea and coffee** – opt for decaffeinated varieties if you drink them a lot, or replace with fruit juice or water occasionally

In addition:
* **Eat a good breakfast** – cereals, fruit or wholemeal toast will give you an energy boost at the start of the day
* **Take time to eat properly** – don't skip meals or eat on the run. Give yourself a break and enough time to digest your food properly
* **Eat a varied diet** – try not to rely on the same menu day after day. The wider the range of foods you eat, the better
* **Avoid snacks** – most tempting snack foods tend to be high in sugar and fat. Whether you eat the traditional three square meals or four or five smaller ones, eat well at your regular meal times so that you don't feel hungry in between

Exercise regularly
Adopting the habit of take a little *regular* exercise will pay big dividends in terms of fitness. It's surprising just how little is required for basic health. Essentially, you need to take care of your:
* **Heart and lungs** – you need some aerobic activity that makes you slightly out of breath. Twenty minutes to half an hour of brisk walking, cycling or swimming three times a week will do. Every day would be even better, and would help to build up your stamina
* **Suppleness** – gentle stretching will help to keep your body free from stiffness, aches and pains. Ten minutes three times a week will keep you in shape, or every morning if you prefer

- **Muscle strength** – include some form of exercise that requires you to use your strength once or twice a week. This could include natural activities such as digging the garden or chopping wood.

As well as taking time for specific exercise, you can also improve your general fitness by being a little more active in your day-to-day activities. Use the stairs instead of waiting for the lift, walk to the shop instead of taking the car, bicycle to work, unwind occasionally by going for a walk instead of sitting watching television.

You can enjoy yourself as well. Dancing, energetic play with children, sport and knock-about games are all excellent ways of maintaining fitness. It is regular, *habitual* gentle exercise that reliably builds stamina, suppleness and strength, however, rather than the occasional weekend splurge.

Rest, relaxation and recreation
There are three main things that contribute to balanced rest and relaxation:
- sleeping well
- waking up refreshed
- staying relaxed during the day

Sleep well
Different people need different amounts of sleep. Some are happy and refreshed after just five or six hours, others feel deprived if they don't get eight or nine. The amount of sleep is less important than its quality. Recharge your batteries and get good quality sleep:
- Aim to get to bed at the same time every night. Your body clock can be thrown by random bed-times and make it harder for you to get to sleep
- Establish a routine for winding down before bed. Read a book, listen to restful music, take a bath, whatever. Your mind and your body will both appreciate clear signals that the time for sleep is approaching

- Avoid caffeine in coffee and tea before bed, and be very cautious with alcohol. Hot milk or herbal teas are preferable, but if you tend to wake in the night to go to the lavatory, avoid late-night drinks altogether
- Avoid eating a heavy meal shortly before going to bed, but don't go to bed hungry either
- Make sure the room where you sleep is:
  - well ventilated
  - not too hot
  - reasonably dark
  - quiet – if noise is a problem, earplugs are a comfortable, effective and economical solution
  - the bed is comfortable and your bedding warm
  - kept just as a bedroom, if at all possible. You need to associate going to bed with going to sleep, so bedrooms that are also used as offices or recreational rooms can sometimes cause problems
- Unless your GP advises otherwise, avoid sleeping pills. Reserve them for short-term use in exceptional circumstances

If you have trouble getting to sleep, or wake soon after dropping off:
- Wait a quarter of an hour or so, then get up and do some undemanding activity for a bit (doing the ironing seems to be very popular)
- If worries or a racing mind are keeping you awake, write down your thoughts on a piece of paper then put it aside with the promise you'll deal with it in the morning
- After a short while, go through your usual winding-down routine and prepare to go to sleep again
- Make sure that you are physically comfortable and that hunger, heat or cold aren't keeping you awake
- Whether you sleep or whether you don't, get up at your usual time the next day rather than sleeping on
- If sleeplessness is a persistent problem, speak to your GP about it

Wake refreshed

Get a good start to your day. Wake up feeling refreshed, relaxed and alert:

- Try to wake up at the same time every day, even on weekends and holidays
- Avoid over-sleeping; it can make you feel heavy and headachy and upset your natural sleep patterns. If you need extra sleep, go to bed earlier rather than sleeping late
- Let your body know it's daytime; give it light, air and movement
  - Open the curtains or turn on lights in winter. Don't try to get dressed and ready in dim lighting, your body will be uncertain whether it's day or still night
  - Get some fresh air. Open the window and take a few moderately deep, slow breaths. (If it's below freezing use caution, a sudden shock of cold air can be harmful to some conditions)
  - Move your body. Gentle, undemanding stretching exercises will release tension and get your blood circulating
  - If you can manage it, fulfil all these requirements by getting out into the fresh air and natural light for a short walk before breakfast

Stay relaxed

Being tense uses up valuable energy. By staying calm and relaxed, you can use that energy more effectively.

Develop the habit of staying relaxed throughout the day:

- Check for tensed muscle every so often. Look for tense stomach muscles, hunched shoulders, an habitual frown, etc. Consciously let those muscles relax
- Check your breathing. Relax your chest by taking a deep breath in and letting it out slowly
- If you're in a situation where you feel yourself becoming stressed, angry or upset, breathe in, counting slowly

to three, and breathe out again before saying or doing anything
- If you're becoming flustered, deliberately slow down and concentrate on using slow, purposeful movements
- Be aware of the things that put extra stress on your body:
  - caffeine in tea, coffee and cola drinks
  - chocolate, sweets and sugar
  - junk food
  - cigarettes
  - alcohol

As well as checking for tension, take time each day to practise consciously relaxing, both physically and mentally.

Each of these exercises takes around five to ten minutes to complete. If you have more time though, take as long as you like. Relaxing music or a tape of natural sounds can also help set the mood.

Physical relaxation
One of the easiest ways to release physical tension is to deliberately tense and relax each group of muscles in turn:
- Sit or lie in a quiet, comfortable place where you won't be disturbed
- Begin by taking a deep breath in and letting it out slowly
- Just enjoy letting go and breathing quietly for a moment
- Beginning with your feet, tense the muscles for a second or two and then let go and release the tension
- Tense the muscles in your legs and then let go
- Continue all the way up your body, tensing and relaxing your muscles
- Finally, squeeze your face muscles into a tight grimace and then let go and relax
- Remain quietly relaxed for a few moments, breathing slowly and gently

Mental relaxation
You can either continue on from the previous exercise

while lying quietly relaxed, or do this separately:

- Make yourself comfortable
- Close your eyes and think of somewhere ideal for relaxing – the beach, perhaps, or a garden
- Imagine you are actually there – enjoy the sights and sounds and scents around you. Feel the warm sun on your skin, hear the gentle waves or the soft rustle of leaves
- If any thoughts intrude, simply notice them and then let them go. Bring your thoughts back to the peaceful place you are imagining
- Imagine your body being refreshed as you enjoy the peace and calm
- After five or ten minutes, open your eyes. Take a deep breath and let it out slowly
- Have a good stretch. Sit up or get up in your own time

Recreation

Recreation is a very simple and often-neglected part of a healthy life. In order to re-charge your batteries, you need to set aside time to:

- Be alone with yourself
- Do things that give you pleasure
- Spend time with people who like you

Be alone with yourself

Take time to get to know yourself. Find out what your own moods and rhythms are when you're away from the influence of other people. You could:

- Take yourself for a walk
- Take yourself away for the day to explore a new place
- Curl up with a good book
- Paint a picture
- Write your diary
- Play old records
- Go through your photograph album

Be kind to yourself, nurture yourself, and plan treats for yourself, just as you would for any other best friend.

Do things that give you pleasure

Doing things you enjoy sounds very obvious, but it's just the sort of thing that gets pushed to the bottom of the list when you're busy or stressed.

Make a list of all the things that give you pleasure, and consciously remind yourself to do them regularly. Include a range of things that are:

- Exciting
  - Adventure – travelling, exploring, trying new things
  - Sports – team games or individual physical activity to enjoy a sense of exhilaration and movement
  - Challenges – physical challenges, running, hiking, climbing, orienteering, sailing
- Creative
  - Exercising your talents – musical, artistic, dramatic, practical, intellectual
  - Going to the theatre, art galleries, cinema
  - Painting, sculpture, photography
  - Writing poetry, fiction, letters, articles
  - Playing music, listening to music
  - Developing crafts
- Stimulating
  - Learning new things – skills, languages, new topics, hobbies and interests
  - Computer games
  - Word games and puzzles
  - Quizzes and competitions
- Rewarding
  - Volunteer work
  - Charity work
  - Community projects
- Practical
  - Gardening
  - Cooking
  - DIY and decorating
- Sociable
  - Family visits and get-togethers

- Time with friends
- Children's activities
- Groups and societies
- Relaxing
  - Meditating
  - Enjoying nature, walking, bird-watching
  - Unwinding, strolling, sitting by the fire, lying in a hammock

Spend time with people who like you

Make sure you see the people whose company you enjoy. This is another of those things that can get overlooked in a busy schedule, but time spent with friends is essential to well-being.

Nurture friends carefully and make the most of your relationships:
- Take a genuine interest in your friends, ask them questions and listen to the answers
- Share their enthusiasm and be glad when they're happy
- Let down your barriers and be open with them
- Be ready to offer and receive support
- Be generous with both apologies and forgiveness when needs be
- Be willing to be forgiven, too
- Be what you would like others to be – loyal, sensitive, discreet, whatever. Display in your own behaviour the qualities that you value in others
- Let your friends know that you like them

SUMMARY

Positive thinkers have energy.

Enhance your natural energy:
- Eat a balanced diet
  - increase your intake of fruit, vegetables and complex carbohydrates
  - decrease your fat intake

- Take regular exercise
  - twenty or thirty minutes, three times a week, minimum
- Get enough rest
- Relax
- Make time for recreation
- Be wary of instant lifts
- Keep stress under control

4
MOTIVATION

WHAT IS MOTIVATION?
Motivation is the urge to achieve aims and reach goals. It's
the persistent drive that gets you through the difficult
patches and impels you to attain your objectives. It's the
ability to maintain an interest, and a sense of direction and
forward movement towards a desired outcome. It's the
underlying, inherent reason why you do anything at all,
ever.

Different people have different motivations, and what
motivates one person can often leave another cold. Your
individual motivation will depend largely on your personal
values, but some of the key factors inherent in the desire to
get something done are:
- **Emotional attraction** – you will rarely persevere with
  something you don't feel strongly about
- **Courage** – a degree of personal courage and per-
  severance are needed to take the initiative and start
  projects, and to overcome obstacles and set-backs along
  the way
- **Optimism** – the positive expectation of a successful
  outcome is needed in order to start in the first place
- **Energy** – feelings of low physical energy and impaired
  resilience quickly sap the will to take action
- **Purpose** – vision and a sense of mission give purpose
  and direction, and help to maintain motivation over the
  long term

WHY IS MOTIVATION USEFUL?
Motivation is what takes dreams and plans and turns them
into reality. Positive thinkers are very good at getting motivated and staying motivated. They have mastered the art of
self-motivation, and use that skill to put their best effort
into whatever they do.

This makes them enviably independent. They are clear about what they want to do and why they want to do it. Because they have a clear idea of how what they want fits in with their values and contributes to their purpose in life, they are able to stick to tasks until they achieve the desired outcome.

Their natural talent for self-motivation means that when they need to boost their self-esteem, they are often able to look back on confidence-enhancing success rather than a string of abandoned projects and half-hearted failures.

DEVELOPING MOTIVATION

Highly-motivated people are often very clear what their values are. Consequently, they know what is likely to motivate them to act in most circumstances. Financial security will be important to one person and, hence, a strong motivating factor. This person will ensure that increased financial security is one of the rewards of a proposed course of action. To another person it could have no meaning at all – their values being based on adventure, say, or their standing in the community.

Look at your values to see where your own motivation lies.

Well-motivated people also have other habits of thought that help you to:
• Get motivated *and*
• Stay motivated

Getting motivated

Optimism, energy and a sense of purpose are an excellent foundation for self-motivation. Setting well-planned personal goals based on your values will help you to keep a sense of purpose – of moving forward and being in control – and maintain an optimistic, positive, up-beat attitude to life.

When you are working on establishing your goals, or planning new ones, remember to build in some motivation for yourself. Do what naturally-motivated people do:

- Focus on the benefits and the rewards
- Build in some feedback
- Enjoy your future
- Know how to troubleshoot

Focus on the benefits and rewards

It's easy to get caught up in anticipating potential problems, hurdles and obstacles when planning objectives. So it's important to take time to imagine, expect and enjoy the positive results of your actions before you start:

- While you're engaged in your task, take a few minutes every day to visualize, as clearly as you can, the outcome you want
- For the purpose of this exercise, focus on the end result rather than the details of how you get there
- If your goal is a better relationship, for example, visualize and enjoy *having* that enjoyable relationship
- Picture in detail what will be happening when you actually achieve that good relationship. Imagine:
  - what you are saying
  - what you are doing
  - most importantly, how you are feeling

Build in some feedback

Success is highly motivating. Make sure that you include recognizable points along the route to your goal that will let you know you're getting there, and give you the chance to celebrate.

Enjoy your future

Take time to appreciate your future and to link it to your present and your past:

- Take time once a week or so to review your life
- Imagine you had an overview of your life. Stand aside from it or float above it, and view it as a whole, focusing on the positive things

- Notice the paths that lead to where you are today
- Notice and appreciate all the positive things that surround you in the present
- Notice the pleasant, positive achievements that await you in the future
- Notice how and where the activities you are embarked on at the moment fit in with your life and form bridges to the future
- Appreciate the things you can look forward to in the future, and add some more if you wish

Troubleshooting

If you're having trouble getting up the motivation to embark on a task or project, or you keep putting it off or are having difficulty getting started:

- Check it against your values and your roles. Is it something you really want to do, or just something you feel you ought to do?
- Is it something you really want to do, or is it just a reaction *against* something else you 'should' or 'ought' to be doing instead?
- Does it interfere with another goal you have? It might run counter to it, or use up time you need to spend on it

To get moving on it:

- Make it a high priority (see 'prioritizing' in Chapter 1, *Sense of Purpose*)
- Break it down into smaller steps until you have a first step you can complete in one operation
- Plan some extra reward for yourself for doing it

Staying motivated

It's easy to stay motivated when things are going well and the rewards are easy to see. It's less easy when:

- you've had a set-back
- your goals seem too far away

Naturally self-motivated people have a number of tricks to help them over obstacles. Try some of them when you encounter set-backs:

Get some support
Make it a life-long project to find people who can encourage you, listen to you and give you practical help or information. Talk through plans, share your dreams, celebrate your successes, and bemoan your failures with them. The secret is to spread the load – don't burden one person with all your problems, and remember to return the favour.

Get some inspiration
Keep small things, souvenirs or a scrapbook, that remind you of past pleasures and personal achievements. Dip into it often. Read about people with a strong sense of purpose or those who have overcome challenges. Find quotes, cuttings and anecdotes that have meaning for you and make a scrapbook from them.

Recall the benefits and rewards
Remind yourself what you will gain by carrying on. Make sure you give yourself time to think about, visualize, anticipate and fully appreciate the outcome you are working for.

Learn from your past
What has motivated you in the past? Popular stimuli that get people moving in the short term include:

competition	altruism	starting a group
praise	fear	doing a class
guilt	affirmations	being dared
treats	revenge	obstinacy
discomfort	curiosity	pride
self-respect	shame	peer pressure
stern lectures	reading about it	

What has worked for you? Make use of anything that has had a positive result to help re-motivate you now.

Learn from the present

What can you learn from the current situation that will be of use to you in the future? What are the positive factors that you can concentrate on? Often, focusing on the positive is all that's needed to re-kindle enthusiasm.

Think about the next stage

What are you looking forward to, what will you enjoy about the next stage of your task or project? Think about what happens after you have got through this difficult part.

After a set-back, you sometimes need something quick to re-motivate you and get you going again. If you need just that little extra to kick-start you into action again:

Give yourself a holiday

Decide what you need to do next, set a time or a date on which you will do it, then give yourself a holiday until that time arrives. Whether it's ten minutes, ten days or ten weeks, take the pressure off and give yourself a complete break during that time.

Do it for five minutes

When a task seems too difficult, too big or too boring, promise yourself that you'll do it for just five minutes (ten minutes if you can bear it) every day. Keep your promise, do it for exactly five minutes and then stop. Either you'll chip away at the task in five-minute bites until the worst is over, or you'll discover during that five minutes that it's not so bad after all.

Succeed at something else

If your motivation is low because of a recent failure, build up your confidence again by doing something you *know* you do well.

Do something practical

If things seem slow, pep yourself up by doing something

with an immediate, definite result where you can see an instant reward for your labour. Cleaning the car, painting a room, turning out cupboards and clearing out the garage are all popular ones.

Do something different

When the set-backs seem impassable and the obstacles insurmountable, consider doing something totally off-the-wall and unpredictable. Try a wild idea, back a wild hunch – or at least give yourself the freedom to imagine what would happen if you did.

Sometimes you can lose motivation for no apparent reason. When you seem to be losing interest in the goals that you've chosen:

- **Check your values** – are you drifting out of line or off-target with your goal? Does it really reflect your values, will it aid your purpose?
- **Check your roles** – things change. Is your goal based on a role you no longer have?
- **Check your goal** – do you still want to achieve it? Or is it something you've outgrown, or satisfied through other means?
- **Is the goal challenging enough?** – if it isn't, upgrade it or move on to something else
- **Is is too challenging?** – break it down into easier steps
- **Are your standards too high?** – perfectionism can get in the way of achievement. Getting it done is often more important than getting it perfect
- **Are you getting negative messages?** – do you feel you're getting disapproval, criticism or lack of interest from people around you? Negative messages can be very de-motivating. Give your detractors the benefit of the doubt and put a generous interpretation on what they say. (See Chapter 2, *Optimism*.) Reward and congratulate yourself for what you have achieved so far, and enlist some better support for the future
- **Is something missing?** – are there obstacles that could be resolved through practical means? Are there skills or

resources that would make things easier? It's surprising how a small practical change can make a big difference.

SUMMARY

Positive thinkers have motivation.

Enhance your natural motivation:
- Look at your values to understand what motivates and rewards you
- Build those rewards into your undertakings
- Focus on the benefits you will gain from your chosen course of action
- Anticipate and enjoy those rewards fully
- Build in feedback to chart your progress towards your goal
- Have some re-motivating tricks up your sleeve in case of set-backs

5

REALISM

WHAT IS REALISM?

Positive thinking is sometimes dismissed as just wishful thinking. True positive thinkers, however, are a long way from being fantasists. Their positive outlook largely relies on their skill of seeing the world as it is and acting accordingly, rather than imagining it as either far better or much, much worse than reality suggests.

WHY IS REALISM USEFUL?

Far from believing that everything will work out all right if you just wish it to, or that anybody can do everything without effort or application, people who naturally think positively understand that:

* it takes times to build up a skill or a reputation
* it takes effort to learn something, create something, build something
* it takes determination to see things through
* it takes patience to see results
* luck mostly happens to people who have already done the groundwork
* this is an imperfect world and you can't count on magic

They remain positive and optimistic not only despite these realizations, but to some extent because of them. With that understanding, they undertake new tasks and projects with a full realization of what they need to put into it, and consequently avoid being disappointed, frustrated or running out of steam halfway through. They appreciate that most success must be earned and they are willing to:

* go into things without holding back for fear of failure
* try new things without expecting to get it right first time
* put in time and effort to get results
* undertake things without expecting perfection

Realism is what stops positive thinkers from turning into fantasists with rose-tinted spectacles. They have a certain toughness and a willingness to take the rough with the smooth.

Developing the skill of realism means they are not afraid to wade in and have a go at things – if they fail, then that's just life and no great tragedy. They rarely see it as failure, though. They focus instead on what they've got right and what they could do differently another time. They learn from the situation.

Realists have the optimism, self-motivation and courage to appreciate that one of the easiest ways to deal with difficulties is to tackle them and get them out of the way as quickly as possible. Without dwelling on the negative, they have a philosophical acceptance of the way the world is, and realize that life is much simpler when you:
- face up to problems
- get the boring or difficult stuff out of the way first
- accept that there are things you've elected to be responsible for
- stop putting things off
- stop hoping they'll just go away

DEVELOPING REALISM
Optimism, energy, purpose and self-motivation are an excellent foundation from which to face the realities of life. To develop that resilient, optimistic realism that characterizes natural positive thinkers, copy some of the habits of natural realists:
- Recognize your mistakes
- Take risks
- Focus on doing, rather than dreaming
- Be honest with yourself

Recognize your mistakes
Everybody has times when they could have done better,

but blaming yourself only undermines your confidence and self-esteem, and makes it harder to try again. Accept that everybody, including you, makes mistakes. Looking at them in a positive light and learning from them puts you in a stronger, more positive position than just trying to avoid any situation where you might make mistakes in future.

Example:
You missed a deadline by not sending in a report on time.

Unrealistic thinking:

Pessimism: 'This always happens to me, I can't ever get anything right.'
              'I'm not right for this job. I can't cope with the demands.'

Rose-tinted: 'It'll be all right, they won't mind. It wasn't that important anyway.'

Realistic thinking:

'It would have been on time if the printer had been working properly. I noticed there was something wrong last week and did nothing about it. I do have a tendency to put things off or leave them until the last moment. I left the details to chance, and then ran into difficulties.'

By being open-minded and realistic about the situation, you can recognize and accept how the problem has come about. You will then be in a strong position to do something positive and practical about it, so there will be fewer similar mistakes in future. Replace your bad habits with positive ones:

- **Decide what you want to change**
  Work out what's at the root of the problem. In the example above, it's the habit of putting things off until they become urgent.
- **Decide what you want to do instead**
  Replace your negative habit with a positive one. Decide

what you would rather do and state it clearly to yourself. Keep it positive – focus on what you *do* want to do rather than what you *don't* want to do. In the above example it could be: 'I want to take positive action on problems as they arise.'

- **Look for opportunities to do it**
  Think about how you are actually going to behave in similar situations in the future. Rehearse it in your imagination and plan what you are going to do. Try it out – be alert for chances to put your new habit into practice.

- **Learn from feedback**
  What happens when you put your new habit into effect? Are there ways you could improve it? Are there times when you slip back into the old habit? How can you get over that?

- **Reward yourself**
  Give yourself a small reward and lots of praise and encouragement whenever you use your new habit. Avoid punishing or scolding yourself if you make a mistake, just think how you could do it better next time.

Take risks

Failure is not the end of the world. Positive thinkers have their steady optimism to pull them through difficulties but, as realists, they also recognize that there are no guarantees in life and you sometimes have to risk failing in order to succeed. While it is tempting to seek comfort and certainty, we need some challenge in order to test our own strength and realize our own potential.

Being adventurous is stimulating, it builds self-esteem and self-reliance, and seems to account for much of the 'stress hardiness' of positive thinkers. Interestingly, in the long term it seems to make little difference whether the outcome is successful or not. It's actually *taking* the risk that's important, rather than ducking out or waiting for the soft option.

Try some small risks that reflect your values and purpose in life:

- **Do things that you enjoy**
  Do things that you enjoy for their own sake, don't worry about success or failure. Risk not being good at what you do, just bring commitment and enthusiasm to it. Do something that you can lose yourself in without being conscious of mistakes or shortcomings.
- **Try new things**
  Taking risks, being adventurous and doing something new all stimulate self-confidence. Attempting something that you have never tried before enhances belief in yourself and your abilities, and helps build up your resources.
  - Book a holiday somewhere unusual but tempting
  - Do a class in something you've never done but might enjoy
  - Apply for a job you're not qualified for
  - Go on a course you're not quite up to and be prepared to work hard
  - Write a letter to a national magazine or newspaper
  - Offer to give a talk on your favourite subject
  - Ring up an acquaintance you'd like to know better
  - Pick up a 'difficult' book and just plough through it
  - Volunteer for something at work
  - Write a short article and send it off to your local paper
  - Join a new club or society
  - Try a type of food you've never eaten before
  - Try a difficult recipe
  - Take another route to work
  - Enrol on an activity holiday you've always wanted to do
  - Book the test, enrol for the exam or try for that qualification you've always put off doing
  - Enter a competition
  - Try a new sport

Focus on doing, rather than dreaming
Realists recognize that one action is worth a thousand

words. While imagining positive outcomes and planning are important first steps, realists understand that in order to achieve anything, above all, they have to *do*. Whatever your goals, take persistent, regular steps, however small, towards completing them. Do something every day, however little, however hard it is:

- **Just do it**
  Above all, you actually have to perform the tasks and activities required to reach your goal. Realistically assess the amount of effort that you will need to put into it and decide if you have the time, self-motivation and enthusiasm necessary. If you decide to go ahead, don't agonize about waiting for the right time, or put it off until you get into the right mood, *just do it*.
- **You don't have to be perfect**
  It doesn't matter how badly you do something at first, just do it regularly. You can expect to do badly and make mistakes when you begin something new and reach out into unfamiliar areas. Be patient with yourself and don't let perfectionism stand in your way. It is persistent and regular *doing* rather than doing *well* that is important.
- **Break everything down into small steps**
  Break tasks down into their component parts and work through each part in turn. Set yourself recognizable targets on the way to completing your goal. Progress towards your goal in small steps rather than trying to do it in one big jump. If, for example, you want to increase the number of sit-ups you can accomplish in a session from five to fifty, aim first for seven a session, then ten, then fifteen, and so on.
- **Look at the results**
  Studying the results of what we do is how we learn, grow, and improve. Look at the feedback and think about the results you are getting as you go along. What did you do well, and what would you do differently another time? You may notice that there are areas that could repay greater concentration, or areas that you

would like to develop further. You may need further
resources, knowledge or information before you can
continue.

- **Congratulate yourself**
  When you achieve a target on the way to your goal
  remember to congratulate yourself. Tell yourself how
  well you are doing, appreciate how it contributes to your
  purpose, and reward yourself in some way. It's tempting
  to think that the achievement itself is the reward, but our
  minds don't always seem to work in that way – we want
  recognition and celebration as well.

Be honest with yourself

Realists are very honest with themselves. They know
themselves well, they value themselves, and they accept that
their happiness and well-being are ultimately their own
responsibility. They acknowledge their mistakes and make
amends for them. They know when they're in the wrong
and apologize fully and generously. They understand when
they are living at odds with their own values and are quick
to put things right.

They also recognize and accept the difference between reasons and excuses, and will rarely allow themselves to hide
behind an excuse without some practical idea of how to
overcome it. Copy their strategies:

Excuse	Strategy
'I've got too much else to do'	• Check your commitments; are you taking on too many roles? Do they *all* fit in with your values?
	• Enlist help; explain what you are aiming to do and ask for practical support
	• Work out your priorities; is what you want to do more important or less important than the things you are already doing?
'I haven't got the time'	• Work expands (and contracts) to fill the time available; is there something you could 'borrow' time from?
	• Work out what you have got time for and do that bit, however little

PERFECT POSITIVE THINKING

	• Plan out a timetable to make the best use of your time
	• Budget your time like money; find out what you spend it on, where you could make savings, where you could invest more
'I haven't got the confidence'	• Nor has anyone else; confidence can only be built up gradually through doing things and learning from your mistakes
	• See Chapter 8, *The Comfort Zone*
'I'm too tired to do it'	• Check your health; see Chapter 3, *Energy* Paradoxically, more exercise could help you to feel less tired
	• Are you tired, or just uninspired? Boredom can feel very much like tiredness
	• If you feel you suffer from more than ordinary levels of tiredness, check with your GP
'I'm not sure it's what I want'	• Check your values and your purpose in life to see how and where it fits in
	• Work out the worst that could happen if you do it, work out how you would recover from it, decide if it's a risk worth taking
	• See Chapter 7, *Indecision*
'What would people say about it?'	• Are the people involved significant people in your life or just generalized, nebulous 'other people'?
	• Find out what those significant people think; talk it over with them
	• Work out the worst that could happen if significant people disapprove of what you do, work out how you would deal with it, decide if the risk is worth taking

Realists are also honest enough with themselves to admit that, sometimes, whatever the reasons, whatever the excuses, there are some things that they just don't *want* to do.

SUMMARY
Positive thinkers have realism.

Enhance your natural realism:
• Accept that things are not always easy, but that doesn't mean that they're invariably dreadful

- Admit that you make mistakes, and learn from them
- Recognize bad habits and replace them with positive ones
- Accept that doing new things is a risk
- Take small, regular steps towards the things you want, even when it's hard
- Be honest with yourself and don't put up with excuses

Part Two:
NEGATIVE BELIEFS

This section looks at the things that may get in the way of developing positive attitudes:

6

NEGATIVITY

WHAT IS NEGATIVITY?

Negativity is the sum total of those negative thoughts, feelings and beliefs that we all have to a greater or lesser extent.

Individually, each thought or feeling would be easy to deal with. However, sometimes we can get caught in a downward spiral where negative thoughts breed negative feelings, which give rise to negative behaviour. The negative feedback we get from the negative behaviour creates more negative thoughts and feelings, and so it goes on.

WHY DOES NEGATIVITY HAPPEN?

We get a lot of negative messages from the world, especially while we are growing up. Parents, teachers, siblings, peers, they all have an effect on us, and we learn early on that life can be a risky, dangerous and disappointing business. We get plenty of negative messages such as:

- Don't expect too much
- Pride comes before a fall
- Don't count your chickens before they are hatched
- Never rest on your laurels, you must always try harder
- You'll be sorry
- The higher you fly, the harder you fall
- Those that ask, don't get
- Don't invite disappointment

They were meant to be helpful but they often left us with the impression, from an early age, that the world is a grudging, capricious, mean-spirited place. The results can be lingering feelings of guilt and unease, a sense of foreboding, and a deep suspicion of doing or saying anything that might tempt fate. After all:

- Little birds that sing in the morning, cry in a ditch at night!

OVERCOMING NEGATIVITY

There are three keys to overcoming negativity:

- Build up a positive image of yourself and the world around you
- Change the negative voice inside your head into a positive one
- Challenge negative feelings with positive ones

Build a positive image

Your image of yourself is largely based on your perception of your individual skills and qualities – what you are, what you do, and how well (or badly) you believe you do it.

Positive people have a very clear idea of what their skills and qualities are. This helps them maintain their self-respect and self-esteem, and gives them a realistic, practical foundation for their goals and purpose in life.

They also have a clear, realistic idea of what their strengths and weaknesses are. They are able to recognize, appreciate and use their strengths, and take steps to correct or modify weaknesses where these may be a hindrance.

Build a positive, realistic picture of yourself. Look at:

- your skills
- your qualities
- your strengths
- your weaknesses

What are your skills?

Your skills are the knowledge and ability that you have acquired and developed over the years. Some skills will be highly practical – typing, driving and book-keeping, for example. Others will be more abstract and intuitive – communicating, negotiating or motivating.

Some skills, perhaps the ones you use at work, will be more highly-developed than others, but everyone has a range of skills – some with people, some with things, others with ideas. Everything we do uses some mixture of skills:

at work	studying	doing crafts
at home	pursuing interests	for fun
with family	pursuing hobbies	with friends
as a partner	pursuing concerns	on your own
as a parent	doing sports	

People who are natural positive thinkers often place a high value on *all* their skills. They see the skills they develop through hobbies such as music or sport, or a role such as parenting, as being just as important as those developed for work.

This gives them a wide range of opportunities to consciously exercise and develop their skills and talents, with the accompanying lift to their self-esteem that might be expected. To develop your positive image of yourself, look at your own skills. What are your abilities? Think about all the things you do, and all the different skills you use:

Examples of skills:

organizing	planning	fund-raising
making	innovating	negotiating
delegating	computing	motivating
communicating	typing	supervising
presenting	leading	travelling
studying	building	creating
repairing	writing	observing
specifying	counselling	reporting
listening	teaching	analysing
driving	accounting	influencing
crafting	budgeting	selling
managing	campaigning	trading

Make a list of all your skills and take the opportunity to reflect on them and enjoy them. Then, looking at each of them in turn, decide whether you want to:

- improve or strengthen it in any way
- add to it in any way
- use it more often
- you're happy with it as it is

Example:

Skill	What to do with it
Management skills	Use more often. Use time-management skills to organize leisure time rather than frittering it away on chores. Use negotiating skills with children rather than bossing them around
Language skills	Add to – develop spoken and written German for increased business use
Photography	Improve – apply for course in September, timetable one weekend a month for day out with camera
Music	Do nothing – just enjoy it as it is

List the things you want to do, such as finding a photography class, getting camera film, planning some days out, borrowing some German language tapes, etc., and as with planning any other sort of goal, think about the steps you need to take to explore or develop your skills.

What are your qualities?
Your qualities are aspects of your character and personality that have developed over a lifetime. Whether you're born with them or acquire them early on, a good self-image depends on recognizing, appreciating and strengthening the qualities that we like in ourselves:

Examples of qualities:

kindness	flexibility	unflappability
intelligence	versatility	efficiency
responsibility	perception	sensitivity
leadership	diplomacy	practicality
understanding	wit	honesty
friendliness	punctuality	persistence
ambition	imagination	energy
dependability	determination	patience

Think about which personal qualities you value and are important to you. List your own qualities and enjoy recognizing them and appreciating them. Then, as you did with your skills, look at each of them in turn and decide whether you want to:

- improve or strengthen it
- add to it in any way
- use it more often
- you're happy with it as it is

Example:

Quality	What to do with it
Versatility	Use more often – try out different ways of doing things instead of relying on the usual approaches
Assertiveness	Improve – find assertiveness course or self-help book
Energy	Add to it – improve diet and go to bed earlier. Do one active thing over the weekend
Patience	Do nothing – content with it as it is

Make a list of the things that you want to do, then plan the steps needed to carry them out.

What are your strengths?

Strengths are the things that you're good at – the mixture of skills and qualities that you feel confident about using.

Write down the things that you do well, and list all the skills and qualities that go with each particular activity.

Example:

I am good at	Skills needed	Qualities needed
Designing and making my own clothes	designing, adapting, planning, budgeting, dress-making	imagination, patience, energy practicality, aesthetics
Producing the company magazine	desk-top publishing, organizing, design, communication, negotiation	tact, responsibility, versatility imagination, wit
Teaching photography	photographic – technical and artistic, teaching, organizing communication, listening, motivating	friendliness, discipline understanding, patience, persistence

Look at your strengths and enjoy them. You can use all these skills and qualities to improve your quality of life and well-being, to have fun and to pursue your life purpose. Are there skills that you could add, or qualities you could develop, that would further enhance your strong points? If there are, what steps do you need to take to acquire them?

What are your weaknesses?

What are the things that let you down and get in the way of your strengths?

Communication, for instance, might be an important skill for a manager. If you were a manager and lacked this particular skill, you would probably want to take steps to develop it. Note any weaknesses you may have and decide whether:

- you want to improve it
- you can get around it or compensate for it
- it's not that important

Example:

Weakness	What to do about it
Poor punctuality	improve it – get alarm clock mended or buy new one. Set watch five minutes ahead and use in-built alarm for appointments
Lack of authority	compensate – use communication skills and qualities of understanding and patience instead
Can't drive	do nothing – it's not that important while I live in the city

List the things that you want to do and plan accordingly.

Plan positive experiences

As well as working on developing a positive self-image, cultivate positive experiences of the world around you:

- Cut out and keep up-beat stories from the press
- Ask friends what they enjoy in life
- Swap stories about the best times you ever had
- Ask them what's going well at the moment

- Ask your family too
- Read biographies and autobiographies about happy, worthwhile people who have fun occasionally
- Keep a list of people who have achieved something against the odds
- Add one name a week to it
- Collect cheerful quotes and sayings and pin them up where you can see them
- Add postcards, pictures, cartoons and photographs that make you smile

Look positive

Even when you don't feel positive, you can always look positive.

It's strange but true that behaving in a positive manner will often make you feel more positive, however you feel when you start. If other people perceive you as more positive, they start to treat you more positively and, with that positive feedback, you actually come to feel more positive yourself.

An easy way to appear positive – confident, friendly and approachable – is suggested by the acronym **SOFT**. This stands for:

Smile	Smile and look cheerful, and other people will respond to you positively.
Open	Use open rather than closed, defensive postures. Hold your head up and keep your shoulders back. Rest your hands in your lap or on the arm of your chair, rather than folding your arms across your chest.
Forward	Look forward and lean forward towards the person you are speaking to, don't back away from them. Face them and make eye contact. Clearly and confidently direct your attention towards them.
Touch	Cultivate a firm, confident handshake for a positive first impression.

Change the negative voice

A lot of us seem to carry a little negative voice around in the back of our minds a lot of the time, criticizing and undermining what we do. Maybe it's an echo of the past, or of our own negative experiences, but overcoming negativity means turning that derogatory voice into an encouraging, supportive one. To do that we need to:

- turn negative labels into positive ones
- turn negative self-talk into positive self-talk

Turn negative labels into positive ones

We often put labels on ourselves and our behaviour, and these labels can be quite negative at times: 'I'm terribly bossy', 'I'm just being lazy', 'You must think I'm awfully old-fashioned', and so on.

Positive people think optimistically and give others the benefit of the doubt, putting the best possible interpretation on their behaviour. They are also able to do the same for themselves. They give their 'negative' traits a positive interpretation, and are able to recognize that there are positive sides even to supposedly undesirable characteristics.

Try replacing some of your negative labels with more positive ones. Many supposed faults have a much more favourable description that could help you to focus on your positive qualities:

Negative label	Positive label
Stubborn	Persistent
Timid	Cautious
Lazy	Relaxed
Old-fashioned	Traditional
Fussy	Attentive to detail
Shy	Sensitive
Aggressive	Determined
Rude	Forthright
Bossy	Responsible
Stuffy	Formal
Loud	Enthusiastic

Thinking about yourself positively and generously helps you to work *with* your character and develop your potential. If you've labelled yourself as stubborn, for example, you may see this as negative and try to play it down. But by doing so, you may not notice that this characteristic is also what encourages you to be persistent and to keep going in the face of set-backs.

Changing the way you label yourself from 'stubborn' to 'persistent' allows you to express the positive aspect of your natural tenacity, while also opening the door to greater flexibility in your behaviour.

Turn negative self-talk into positive self-talk

Stop the self-critical talk that we all indulge in at times. We are often our own harshest critics, but frequent criticism saps self-confidence and makes it difficult to feel either optimistic or positive.

When you catch yourself making negative judgments about yourself or your performance, stop and think what the generous interpretation would be. Replacing negative comments with more positive ones allows you to, optimistically and realistically, learn from experience and try again.

Negative statements	Positive statements
I did something terrible	I made a mistake
I'm no good	I'm OK
I can't do this	This will take time and concentration
They won't like me	They'll probably think I'm OK
I *must* do better	I *could* improve by doing it differently
I'm a clumsy idiot	I just tripped over
I ought to try harder	I'm doing well in the circumstances

Avoid negative experiences

Where possible, avoid situations that you know are going to be negative unless you have very clear reasons for staying. In particular, avoid indulging in:

- negative conversations – gossip, backbiting, etc.
- doom, gloom and despair in the press
- people who want to complain about everything
- people who want you to share their feeling of helplessness
- people who want to compete for the worst thing that happened to them
- people who want you to share their bad health habits
- biographies and autobiographies about miserable, desperate people who never have any fun
- people who always run other people down
- miserable songs
- depressing stories, plays and films about people without hope

Challenge negative feelings

We all have negative feelings at times and, surprisingly, negative feelings are actually quite useful. When they arise naturally and appropriately, they tell us when something in our world is not as it should be and needs attention. Fear, for example, primes us for fight or flight when we are threatened. Anger alerts us that something unjust or unfair is happening.

The primary negative feelings are:
- Fear
- Grief
- Jealousy or envy
- Anger

Problems arise when these valuable signals linger on past their usefulness. Anger settles down into habitual bad temper or aggression, fear becomes the established response to any and every situation, grief dwindles into apathy and disillusionment.

Rather than letting them take root, combat persistent negative feelings with:

- Courage
- Cheerfulness
- Self-esteem
- Assertiveness

Courage and fear

The good news about fear is:

- **Fear is natural**

  Fear is the unavoidable consequence of having a nervous system designed to keep us safe and out of danger.

- **Fear is useful**

  It alerts us to danger and gets our bodies ready for fight or flight – increased heart-rate, rapid breathing, and so on.

- **Fear can be controlled**

  Courage isn't the absence of fear, it just means over-coming the fear and either tackling the cause of alarm, or carrying on despite it, whichever is appropriate.

Develop your natural courage:

- **Relax**

  Take time regularly to relax both physically and mentally, to keep yourself calm and prevent stress. (See Chapter 3, *Energy*.)

- **Tackle the source of your fears**

  When you relax and look at your fears realistically and objectively, is there some foundation to them? Are there practical things you could do to alleviate them? You may, for example, be right to fear public speaking if you've had no training and very little practice at it, and sensible to worry about burglars if your home has proved insecure in the past. Practical remedies to both these problems are readily apparent.

- **Change the voice in your head**

  Adopt a positive attitude. Instead of telling yourself: 'This is frightening', 'I'm too scared', 'I can't do this', etc., use positive statements like 'This is challenging', 'I'm excited', 'Adrenaline improves my performance',

'This is an adventure', 'I'm alert and in control here'.
- **Tackle fears step-by-step**
  Start with the easiest, least frightening things and work your way up. Remember to reward yourself every time you accomplish something new.

Cheerfulness and grief

Grief is a painful but inevitable part of a full life. Naturally positive people learn to deal with is sensitively and fittingly, rather than trying to avoid it and thereby restricting their lives unreasonably. They realize that:

- **Grief is an entirely natural reaction to loss**
  The grief we feel when something is gone is in proportion to its value and importance to us. To go through life without ever grieving would be to go through life without ever valuing anything, or thinking anything important.

- **Grief is healing from the wound, not the wound itself**
  Although it is understandably painful, grief is actually a healing process and not a wounding one. The pain will heal more quickly and thoroughly if grief is allowed its full expression through tears, talking about the loss, remembering and mourning.

- **Grief is a process**
  It has a beginning, a middle and – although it may not seem like it at the time – an end. Grief becomes a negative rather than a healing force when, for whatever reason, the process becomes stuck and we can't move on beyond it.

Near the end of the grieving process, a time comes when it is natural and appropriate for cheerfulness to start springing up again. Never feel that you have to cling on to unhappiness for any reason.

Even if you don't quite feel like it, give laughter at least an opportunity to break in on a regular basis:

- Search out comedy programmes on television and radio
- Borrow 'comedy classic' tapes from the library
- Choose to rent light-hearted videos rather than serious ones
- Read books and magazines you find funny
- See people who you know you can have a laugh with
- Do things that are fun and make you laugh
- Listen to up-beat music during the day. Even if it's not the sort of thing you would usually listen to, try the local library for light classics and cheerful, popular pieces to lift your spirits

Self-esteem and envy

Envy and jealousy get a very bad press these days. However, the good news about envy is:

- **Envy is natural**
  Few of us have everything we want or secretly think we deserve. Seeing others succeed can spark off feelings that have their roots deep in infancy, when getting what we needed was, quite literally, a matter of life or death.
- **Envy is useful**
  Envy can be a clear signal about what we want in our lives – you only envy in others what you value yourself.
- **Envy can be channelled into useful directions**
  If you use envy as the spur to making positive, productive changes in your own life, then a touch of it can prove useful. It becomes very negative, however, when it turns to unproductive brooding and resentment of others.

Avoid the negative envy trap by building a solid foundation of self-esteem:

- **Nurture your self-esteem**
  Review and build on your skills and strengths in the ways suggested earlier in this chapter.
- **Turn negative talk into positive talk**
  Change the internal voice that says 'It's not fair', 'I should have that', 'It's easy for him/her', 'I never wanted

it anyway!' to one that says 'That's something I could have', 'I expect he/she worked hard for that', 'I'd like that, too', 'I could achieve that', 'That's worth making the effort for'.

- **Set and achieve goals that you value**
  Build a foundation of achievement for yourself, one that is meaningful to you in the light of your values and purpose, and you need never envy anyone anything.

Assertiveness and anger
The good news about anger is:

- **It's natural**
  Anger is a natural response to a threat to our well-being.
- **It's useful**
  Anger can give us the energy to do something about whatever it is that threatens us.
- **It can be controlled**
  The energy of anger, properly handled, can be channelled into productive activity to improve the situation.

To channel the anger and develop your assertiveness:

- **Relax**
  Take time regularly to relax both physically and mentally, to keep yourself calm. (See Chapter 3, *Energy*.)
- **Tackle the source of your anger**
  Where anger is the signal that something is wrong, look at what is making you angry realistically and objectively. Is there something practical you can do about it?
- **Change the voice in your head**
  Adopt a positive attitude. Instead of telling yourself, 'This is unbearable', use positive statements like 'I can keep calm and deal with this'.
- **Release pent-up anger safely:**
  Release it physically
  Physical release of the tension associated with anger, frustration and aggression can be very beneficial. Bottling up emotions is harmful, but so is expressing them destructively. Release tension safely through:

- strenuous exercise – running, swimming, aerobics, anything vigorous
- competitive sport – team games can provide a regular outlet
- hard physical labour – digging the garden, scrubbing floors, chopping wood, sawing logs
- shouting – choose somewhere harmless, or shout into a pillow
- pillow punching, which can be combined with shouting

Release it emotionally

Anger creates emotional as well as physical tension. Bottling it all up can be harmful, but just letting go and saying things better left unsaid can be damaging to relationships and harm your self-respect. Express anger safely:

- Write letters – express your grievances fully and comprehensively, get all your anger and hurt out on to the paper. These letters are not for sending to anyone so you can say whatever you like. *Remember to destroy them afterwards, though.*
- Make a list of all the things you feel angry about – put it all down on paper.

    Example:

    I am angry with the children for being naughty

    I am angry with Tony because he wouldn't take me seriously

When you've finished, look back over your list and decide what you would rather have happened in each case. This helps you to think more calmly about what has actually made you angry.

    Example:

    I would have preferred the children to be quiet and reasonable

    I would have preferred Tony to have listened to me seriously

Is there anything you can do, now that you're calm rather than angry, that would change the situation? Would talking to the person involved, for example, help them to under-stand why you are angry? Could you negotiate anything different in the future? Could you behave differently?

- **Decide your rights**

  Think about the situations where you tend to get angry, and write a list of the things that you feel nobody has the right to do to you.

  > *Example:*
  > Nobody has the right to tell me what to do
  > Nobody has the right to treat me as second rate
  > Nobody has the right to ignore me

  Look back over your list and decide what this means that *you* have a right to.

  > *Example:*
  > I have a right to my independence
  > I have a right to be taken seriously
  > I have a right to be treated well

  This might help you to see the root of your resentment more clearly, and to understand where your self-esteem might be under threat. You can then begin to think clearly about how to change things.

- **Talk it over with someone**

  Choose someone who you think will listen to you with-out interrupting or telling you what to do. Ask them first if they are willing to listen, but don't be hurt if they say they can't; some people do find it very difficult. Just ask someone else.

- **Laugh**

  Laughter can release both the physical and the emotional tension of anger and restore your sense of perspective. Take all the opportunities you can to laugh. Watch comedy programmes on television, spend time with people who can let go and be silly, play with children, read books and magazines you find funny.

SUMMARY

Overcome negativity:

- Develop your self-esteem:

- Know what your skills and qualities are
- Develop them further
- Understand your strengths and work with them
- Understand and deal with your weaknesses
- Change your negative labels into positive ones
- Cut out the negative self-talk
- Pursue positive experiences and avoid negative ones
- Understand your negative emotions and learn to channel them positively. Counter:
  - Fear with courage
  - Grief with cheerfulness
  - Jealousy with self-esteem
  - Anger with assertiveness

7

INDECISION

WHAT IS INDECISION?

People who are natural positive thinkers are, on the whole, clear and decisive about what they want to do and what they want to happen. This is a natural result of their sense of purpose and optimism.

However, even the most confident, assertive, positive people can be familiar with indecision. Sometimes it's hard to be decisive about what to have for lunch, let alone long-term life goals. Usually though, the bigger the impact the decision will have, the harder it is to reach it. It can sometimes seem easier to just let things take their own course and hope for the best.

Indecision usually happens when you have to choose between two or more options:

- You can't choose because all the options look equally attractive or unattractive
- You make a choice but keep changing your mind about it
- You make a choice but, for some reason, are reluctant to put it into effect
- You can't make a choice because there don't seem to be any options to choose from
- The option you'd like isn't open to you, so you have to choose between 'second-best' options
- You didn't realize you had a choice so didn't explore any other options until it was too late

WHY DOES INDECISION HAPPEN?

Indecision is often linked to a lack of purpose. If you have no clear direction and little sense of what you want your future to be, then making decisions can be very hard.

Lack of realism, too, can lead to feelings of either hopeless pessimism – 'it doesn't matter what I want, things never go right for me anyway' – or rose-tinted false optimism – 'why choose? Things will work out all right somehow, they always do'.

Even with purpose and realism, though, decision-making can still be difficult. There are all sorts of reasons why indecision can subconsciously appear to be, at least in the short term, the easier option:

- **Fear**
  Making a decision about something can bring up various fears:
  - fear of failure – of not making the right choice
  - fear of commitment – of having to say goodbye to all the other options
  - fear of getting it wrong – classic procrastination, putting off a decision while gathering more and yet more data
  - fear of criticism – of making a choice that others will disapprove of
- **Rescue fantasies**
  This is another type of fear really, fear of responsibility. The feeling that it would be much better if someone else would make the decision, or make the need to decide unnecessary, can be very tempting. It can also breed feelings of resentment when no such rescue materializes.
- **Perfectionism**
  The idea that there is only one right way to do something, and that you somehow have to work out what that is, is very inhibiting.
- **Lack of practice**
  Young people particularly, but older ones too, sometimes get very little practice in making their own decisions and in assessing and choosing their own options. Somebody else usually does it for them, especially when it comes to major events. Suddenly finding their future in their own hands can be very daunting.

- **Pseudo-indecision**
  Sometimes you know exactly what you should do, but just don't want to do it. This can disguise itself as indecision and feel just as uncomfortable as the real thing.

WHY IS INDECISION A PROBLEM?

Many people never get around to making decisions about their lives just because of those uncomfortable feelings of fear. Unhappily, any natural sense of purpose soon gets lost in the subsequent random drift of events. Optimism may be swallowed up in feelings of frustration and futility, energy without direction can turn destructively inwards, and it is rarely possible to remain motivated by choices in which you have little faith.

It's difficult to feel positive regarding a future about which you've made few choices, and over which you feel you have little or no control. While there is no fool-proof way of unerringly making the right choice, greater confidence in decision-making can lead to increased autonomy and a more positive attitude.

The natural realism of positive people accepts that:
- not all decisions turn our perfectly
- you can never foresee *all* the consequences
- you will never have *all* the data you need
- you will sometimes change your mind, and not always for logical reasons
- even bad decisions can turn out well

OVERCOMING INDECISION

Build on your natural decisiveness and determination. Follow the advice in Part One:
- Get a clear picture of yourself and your purpose in life – where you're going and what you're doing
- Understand your values and, consequently, what motivates you

- Make sure tiredness and stress aren't the root cause of your hesitancy
- Look at what's positive and interesting about opportunities before focusing on what's negative
- Look for solutions rather than dwelling on the problems
- Be realistic about how much you are prepared to put into any situation
- Be prepared to risk trying something new
- Be honest with yourself about the source of your indecision

If you are still having trouble reaching a decision about something, try going through a structured decision-making process based on your values, to select the option that's right for you:

Stage 1 – check your values
- First, list all your options
- Next, list your values and put them in order – most important first
- Compare each option with your values
- Take the two or three options that best fit your values and move on to stage two

Stage 2 – apply optimism
- Take your top two or three options
- List the drawbacks to each option
- Apply optimistic, solution-focused thinking and list all the possible solutions to these drawbacks
- Pick the option with the most practical solutions

This exercise should put you in the position of knowing which options fit your values best, and which one will be the most practical to put into effect.

List all your options
Take time to think about this stage and put down *all* the possibilities, not just the most obvious ones, the ones you

feel you ought to do, or the first ones that come to mind.

Example:
Paula has had a job as a designer with a prestigious company for four years. She is ambitious and anxious to move ahead and a position in management has arisen. She stands an excellent chance of getting it – should she apply for the post?

These were her most obvious options:
• Stay in the same position
• Apply for the management job

Thinking about it further, she came up with some more options:
• Apply for a design job in another company
• Go back to college to undertake further study
• Set up own business

List your values and put them in order
Take the values that you listed for Chapter 1, *Sense of Purpose*, and put them in order of importance to you.

Next, give each value points according to its position. If you have ten values, for example, give your top value ten points, your next highest nine points, and so on down to your lowest value which will have only one point.

Example:
Paula's values are:
• Freedom
• Creativity
• Challenge
• Variety
• Innovation
• Simplicity
• Independence

In order of importance they are:

Value	Points
Creativity	7
Independence	6
Innovation	5
Variety	4
Challenge	3
Freedom	2
Simplicity	1

Compare each option with your values

Alongside each option, list each value that it satisfies together with the number of points you have given it. Add up the total points. The highest scoring options will be the ones that most clearly suit your own personal values.

Example:

For each of Paula's options:

Option	Values satisfied	Points	Total
Stay in same job	Creativity	7	
	Variety	4	
	Challenge	3	
	Simplicity	1	15
Apply for management job	Challenge	3	
	Variety	4	
	Innovation	5	12
Apply for another design job	Creativity	7	
	Variety	4	
	Challenge	3	14
Go back to college	Creativity	7	
	Challenge	3	
	Innovation	5	
	Freedom	2	
	Variety	4	21
Set up own business	Creativity	7	
	Challenge	3	
	Innovation	5	
	Variety	4	
	Independence	6	25

Clearly, a move into management would not be in Paula's interests. If her values had been different, though, the result would have been different too. Had her top values been money, security and prestige, for instance, her best options might well have included taking promotion.

From her original options – stay in the same job or apply for the new post – staying in her present job would suit her better than applying for the management job. Going back to college or setting up her own design business, however, would be even better choices.

Take your top two or three options and list the drawbacks

List the down-sides to each option. This may seem rather negative and not at all the sort of thing a positive thinker should be doing, but realistically acknowledging the drawbacks pulls them out into the open and helps to start the process of looking for solutions – a very positive activity.

Example:

Paula's best options are either going back to college or starting her own business:

Option	Drawback
Going back to college	Lack of money
	Finding new job after training
Starting own design business	Financial insecurity
	High workload
	Stress
	Learning business skills

List the solutions

Once you have the drawbacks in front of you, apply solution-focused optimism to finding ways to counter them.

Even if, by this stage, you feel a clear winner is emerging, it can still be a positive activity to list all your solutions for all your options. This way, you will definitely be choosing the option that suits you best rather than, rather negatively, just avoiding the option that seems to have most problems.

When you know that you *could*, if you wanted, select any of your options, you can genuinely make a free decision about the one that you want.

Example:
Paula's solutions:

Option	Drawback	Solution
Going back to college	Lack of money	Save very hard for next six months Find freelance projects Work during holidays
	Find new job after training	Use college course as springboard for networking
Starting own design business	Financial insecurity High workload	Plan, budget, save Budget time efficiently Drop inessentials during start-up phase Consider setting up with someone else
	Stress	Learn to relax
	Learning business skills	Find short, practical course about self-employment

Paula can now make an absolutely free choice about what she wants to do with her future. In the end, she decides that going back to college to continue her specialized training to a higher level will be the most satisfying option. It satisfies many of her highest priority values – creativity, freedom and challenge, and she sees it offering her a greater probability of independence, innovation and variety in the future than starting her own business might do just at present.

Paula can go ahead with her decision knowing that it reflects her values and her sense of purpose in life. She can direct her energy into setting goals and drawing up detailed plans for achieving them with a high degree of motivation and an optimistic, positive belief in her future.

SUMMARY

Overcome indecision:

- Find out what your options are
- Check them against your values
- Pick the options that match your values best
- Anticipate any potential problems and find solutions
- Go ahead and make an informed, rational choice

8
THE COMFORT ZONE

WHAT IS THE COMFORT ZONE?
There are many situations and experiences we have
encountered so often that we know exactly how to behave
and respond in them, and feel completely at home with
them. This is the comfort zone – the sum of all the things
we have done so often that we feel thoroughly comfortable
about doing them again.

We spend most of our time in this comfort zone, doing
familiar things. We feel competent and confident there, safe
and unchallenged, if sometimes a little bored, unstretched
or restricted. The comfort zone can turn into a comfort
trap, however.

HOW DOES THE COMFORT TRAP HAPPEN?
Finding ourselves faced with the need to do something new
or unfamiliar, we can feel out of our depth. The risk we
perceive can make us feel:
- anxious
- irritable
- angry
- fearful
- helpless
- guilty
- resentful

Naturally, if these negative feelings are strong enough, they
can outweigh any thought of the rewards that the new
experience may bring. This leaves us with just the option of
doing something familiar, trapped in the comfort zone,
afraid to venture out.

However much we want the positive results, the negative
feelings come to mind first when we think about doing

something new. Gradually, we come to automatically associate those negative feelings with the idea of doing something different. The answer? Don't do anything different, and you won't have those negative feelings!

Unfortunately, it's virtually impossible to pursue a life purpose from the safety of the comfort zone. Most goals require you to do something new or unfamiliar, and you have to risk making mistakes and even failing if you want to acquire new skills and proficiencies.

WHY IS THE COMFORT ZONE A PROBLEM?

The comfort zone itself is no problem. The problem starts when we have to do, or want to do, something that lies outside it. Something new that we haven't done before, or something we've failed at before. Something that makes us feel uncomfortable.

Naturally positive people use their comfort zone as a launch pad to wider experiences. They work steadily outwards from what feels comfortable, using what they feel familiar with, and competent in, as a firm foundation to build on.

Being realistic, they don't expect things to always be easy and comfortable, and are willing to put up with the temporary discomfort of those negative feelings in order to experience greater feelings of comfort and satisfaction in the long run. The comfort zone is always there for them when they want to rest, relax or recoup their resources, so taking risks becomes less risky.

A valuable consequence of this is that their comfort zone actually increases in size as they become familiar with, and at ease with, a wider and wider range of situations and experiences. By risking discomfort they, paradoxically, achieve even greater comfort.

OVERCOMING THE COMFORT ZONE

First, build on your natural courage and intrepidity:

- Understand what is important to you, what you believe is worth taking the risk for
- Break big goals down into small, manageable steps only just outside your comfort zone
- Get plenty of rest and relaxation, don't let stress build up
- Focus on your successes
- Minimize your failures
- Look for what's positive and interesting in new opportunities before looking for what might be negative
- Think about the solutions whenever you anticipate problems
- Take time to appreciate the rewards and benefits of doing something new, rather than focusing only on the initial feelings of discomfort
- Know how to learn from your mistakes rather than fearing them
- Stick with it; doing something regularly will take the sting out of it, even if it seems hard at first
- Don't accept excuses from yourself

In addition to the above, there are three main keys that will help you to step outside your own comfort zone:

- Confront your fears
- Build up your confidence
- Take reasonable risks

Confront your fears

The first step in getting outside the comfort zone is to recognize that it's there, and that doing anything new or different can cause negative feelings simply because it *is* new and different, and not because there is anything wrong with doing it.

It's also important to realize that feeling anxious, fearful, helpless, etc., isn't the end of the world, it's just a temporary state. If you can learn to tolerate a degree of discomfort, you will find that it eventually becomes much less threatening altogether. You may even find that positive feelings such as excitement and anticipation have the chance to break through.

Always check back with your values, though. Make sure your reluctance is due only to anticipated discomfort, and not because you are doing something contrary to your beliefs.

Confronting your fears means sorting out your priorities and making choices – is it more important to you to achieve your goal or avoid anxiety? Either choice is valid. Sometimes avoiding anxiety may be a high priority for looking after yourself, at other times pursuing your goals will be more important. There is a difference, though, between making a conscious, reasoned choice and unconsciously reacting out of fear of discomfort.

Build up your confidence

First, let go of your past. Put all your bygone fears, mistakes, embarrassments, anxieties and miscalculations into perspective:

- **Forgive yourself your past mistakes**
  Mistakes are just an essential part of learning to do anything new. They are a stepping-stone to present and future success. Be tolerant and forgiving of past misunderstandings and errors.
- **Look at your past through adult eyes**
  The chances are, the mistakes you made in the past were due to inexperience. You will probably never make those same mistakes again because you are that much more mature and experienced. As you became experienced and mature through having made those very mistakes, you can afford to look back on your younger self with understanding and patience.
- **Look at your past with generosity and kindness**
  Many people are far harder on themselves than they are

on anyone else. Treat yourself with at least the compassion that you would have for a friend or colleague.

Next, build up your courage:

Plan a confident start to the day
Set your alarm fifteen or twenty minutes earlier to give yourself time for the following activities:

- **Wake up fully**
  Get some daylight, fresh air and gentle movement first thing and get off to an optimistic, energetic start. (See Chapter 3, *Energy*.)

- **Smile**
  Strange as it may sound, a false smile can have exactly the same enlivening effect on the brain and body as a real one. Smile at yourself in the mirror first thing, and set yourself up for the day.

- **Try an affirmation**
  An affirmation is a positive statement that you repeat to yourself. Used diligently, they effectively replace the negative self-talk that most of us indulge in. Repeat an up-beat, positive affirmation to yourself while you get ready for the day. Possible ones include:
  - I'm looking forward to today with confidence and enthusiasm
  - I'm looking out for all the good things today brings
  - I enjoy the surprises life brings
  - I trust life
  - I enjoy life

- **Have a healthy breakfast**
  Eat a good breakfast to give you energy for the day ahead. To give your spirits a lift, try listening to cheerful music while you eat instead of listening to the news or reading the paper.

- **Establish your day's priorities**
  Take a few minutes to decide what you want to achieve for the day – what is important, what you want to do and when you intend to do it.

Finish your day off positively

Having had a good start to the day, set aside a few minutes to end it equally well:

- **Review the good things**

  Before you go to sleep, go over the good points of the day, the things you've enjoyed and the things you've learned. Firmly push any anxieties to one side by promising yourself you'll deal with them tomorrow.

- **Look forward to something**

  Think of one thing you intend to enjoy tomorrow.

- **Repeat an affirmation**

  Lull yourself to sleep with a gentle affirmation:

  - I rest deeply and peacefully
  - I have done well and can now rest fully and completely
  - My days are complete and enjoyable
  - All is as it should be
  - All is well

Take reasonable risks

Stepping out of your comfort zone means taking some well-calculated risks. You risk:

- feeling uncomfortable
- making mistakes
- being out of your depth
- doing things that are unfamiliar

Minimize the stress of risk-taking. Keep moving outwards and expanding your comfort zone, without over-burdening your ability to cope:

- **What is the worst that can happen?**

  Before taking any sort of risk, decide what the worst possible thing that could result from it would be, and plan what you would do if that happened. How would you recover?

- **Take things step by step**

  Plan thoroughly and break things down into small steps rather than trying to achieve everything at once.

- **Establish your minimum**

  Surprisingly, it's not the big steps that are the most important, it's just the willingness to do *something* that moves you outside your comfort zone. If you are hesitating about taking some course of action, ask yourself what is the minimum you would be willing to do?

Examples:

Task outside my comfort zone	Minimum I would be willing to do
Speaking in public	Read a short, prepared introduction for a guest speaker
Writing a novel	Sit and write for twenty minutes a day every day
Apply for a new job	Talk to a couple of professional colleagues about what's happening in the industry

If a step outside your comfort zone seems impossible or too uncomfortable to contemplate, keep breaking it down into gentler and gentler stages until you reach something you feel happy with. When you've tackled that successfully, ask yourself what's the next minimum you'd be prepared to do.

- **Don't wait to be rescued**

  You'll be disappointed, and suffer uncomfortable feelings of resentment and frustration when it doesn't happen. Go out and live instead. Go after what you want, rather than waiting for it to drop into your comfort zone.

- **Keep a balance**

  Your comfort zone is there for you to renew your energies in. Balance excitement with routine, challenge with familiarity, and stimulation with rest and ease.

- **Know how to bounce back**

  When mistakes and miscalculations occur, know how to cope with them. The worst way is to ignore the problem, run away from it, or pretend that nothing is wrong. The best way is to acknowledge the mistake and propose a way of rectifying it. Handling mistakes effectively is usually a matter of experience – the more you make the better you get at it.

- **Enjoy your courage**
  Close your eyes and recall a time when you tried something new or unfamiliar that worked out well. Enjoy re-living the experience in your imagination. Enjoy recreating the invigorating feelings you had then, and look forward to experiencing them again in the future.

SUMMARY

Overcome your dependence on the comfort zone:

- Confront your fears and put them into perspective
- Be tolerant of your mistakes and failures
- Put yourself in a courageous frame of mind each morning
- Put yourself in a positive frame of mind each evening
- Learn how to take the stress out of risk-taking

WHAT IS HURRY SICKNESS?

Hurry sickness, crisis addiction, urgency syndrome – whatever you call it, it means you end up dashing wildly from one appointment to another without time for lunch, working late to meet last-minute deadlines, and putting friends and family on hold while you schedule in yet another meeting.

The 'symptoms' of hurry sickness can include:
- A reluctance to stop and think
- Restlessness and sudden boredom
- Impatience with details
- A disinclination to plan effectively and thoroughly
- Crises that crop up with more than normal frequency
- Unease at the thought of being 'idle'
- Panic at the thought of being alone with nothing to do
- No time to spare for anything less than very urgent tasks
- An inability to distinguish between what is urgent and what is important
- Constantly doing two or three things at once
- Inability to give full, focused attention to anything for long
- Reluctance to 'waste time' looking after yourself
- Lack of interest in anything outside immediate concerns and problems
- The temptation to cram 'just one more thing' into the schedule
- Frequently running late for appointments
- Seeing yourself as a 'fire-fighter' or 'troubleshooter'

WHY DOES HURRY SICKNESS HAPPEN?

Although it sounds very different from the comfort trap, hurry sickness serves a very similar purpose: security.

It prevents the sufferer from ever having to examine their life and take the risk of going after what they truly want. If you can cram your life with crises, you will never have time, even if you briefly have the inclination, to think about whether your life is purposeful or happy. You're busy, and that's all that matters.

Being busy makes all of us feel important and useful. We're needed, we don't know how they'd manage without us, and that's very validating. However, rather than just being busy, we could be even more useful if we put that effort into planning and doing things that fit our values, purpose and roles in life. Finding your life purpose may not be urgent, but it is important.

WHY IS HURRY SICKNESS A PROBLEM?

If you always do what's urgent, you will never get around to doing what's important. Responding to instant crises takes the centre of control out of your hands and leaves the direction your life takes entirely up to random outside forces. Without that feeling of control, not only is life ultimately aimless, but stress is also a real problem.

Natural positive thinkers have purposeful, complete lives, yet rarely seem harassed or rushed. They take more risks than average, and often accomplish a great deal, yet seldom appear frazzled by crises. They are nearly always able to distinguish clearly between what is urgent and what is important and they can prioritize accordingly. They can pace themselves without feeling the need to rush, and they are quite prepared to delegate and even say no when necessary.

OVERCOMING HURRY SICKNESS

From an overall change of pace, follow the examples in Part One:

- Find out what is important to you
- Learn to make it a high priority
- Make plans and set goals and targets for yourself

- Understand what else motivates you, besides urgency
- Aim for a healthy, balanced lifestyle that includes rest and recreation
- Learn how to replace bad habits with positive ones
- Be honest with yourself

When you're in the grip of hurry sickness, it's very difficult to understand that it is almost entirely self-generated, especially as crises and urgencies crop up from time to time in everybody's life.

Try letting go of some of the urgency and see what happens, though. Tackle it step by step, starting with something easy – maybe stopping for a twenty-minute lunch break every day – and working your way up. Remember to reward yourself when you achieve a target – stopping for a lunch break five days out of five, for example.

Here are some ways you could tackle slowing down:
- **Establish priorities**
  Read the section on prioritizing in Chapter 1, *Sense of Purpose*. Your highest priorities are those things that reflect your values and are a part of the roles you play. Think seriously about all the urgent crises that crop up that have nothing to do with either. How do they come about? Why are they your responsibility?
- **Look after yourself**
  See Chapter 3, *Energy*, and make time to eat, sleep and take exercise. Schedule in the bare minimum and work up from there – even a little bit is always better than nothing.
- **Plan**
  At the very least, take five minutes every morning to *write down* a list of your top priorities (real priorities – things that are important, not just urgent) for the day, and a schedule into which they can be slotted.
- **Allow more time than you think you need**
  Allocate half as much time again to any undertaking –

from finishing a report, to getting to the station, to making friends with a new neighbour.

- **Prepare**
  Think through jobs and courses of action before you start. Ensure that you have the time and all the resources you need, rather than having to crisis-manage running out of either in the middle.

- **Focus on one thing at a time**
  Concentrate on the task in hand. Relax and breathe slowly and deeply when you feel the urge to abandon it for something else. Do it well, do it thoroughly, and finish it before moving on to something else.

- **Let things develop at their own pace**
  Resist the urge to push plans and relationships. Watch and listen for feedback before proceeding to the next stage. In particular, listen to other people when they talk, and let conversations develop at their own pace.

- **Take time to relax**
  Probably the hardest thing. Start with five minutes a day, scheduled for the same time every day – don't wait until you have a spare moment, or until you feel like it. When it's time to relax just close your eyes and do nothing for five minutes precisely. Reward yourself when you achieve it seven days out of seven.

- **Cut something out**
  Even harder to do than taking time to relax, and definitely well on the way to living without hurry sickness. Start easing out all the things that don't relate to your life-purpose and values. Set yourself clear targets – aim to cut one meeting a week out of your schedule, for example, or hand over your club treasurer's position to someone else by the end of the year. Reward yourself when you achieve a target, and move on to the next one.

SUMMARY

Overcome hurry sickness:
- Shift your focus from what's urgent to what's important

- Slow down and take time to concentrate on what you're doing
- Think and plan ahead rather than waiting for crises to dictate what you should be doing
- Time spent looking after yourself is never wasted

10

DEMAND THINKING

WHAT IS DEMAND THINKING?

Sometimes, particularly when things are most important to us, we become rather tense and inflexible about getting what we want – we *demand* that a thing should be so rather than *preferring* that it should be.

We *must* get what we want; it would be *awful* if we didn't.

We *must not* have to go through this; it would mean the end of the world.

It *must* happen; we can't bear it otherwise.

We *have* to have that; it's unthinkable otherwise.

We set up expectations and make demands on ourselves, other people and life in general that almost guarantee disappointment. Going after the things we want becomes a risky business fraught with frustration, tension and distress, rather than the pleasurable, satisfying, light-hearted activity that it should be.

In particular, we often unconsciously demand that:
- Effort *must* be rewarded (and it's *awful* when it's not)
- We *must* be considered and respected (and it's *dreadful* when we're not)
- Love, kindness, goodwill, etc. *must* be returned (and it's *terrible* when they aren't)
- Things *must not* be too difficult (and it's *intolerable* when they are)
- We *must not* suffer discomfort (and it's *unbearable* if we have to)

WHY DO DEMANDS HAPPEN?

It's understandable why we're so demanding. When we were babies, tiny and nearly helpless, our needs were very straightforward and getting them met was, literally, a matter of life and death. As babies we *must* have food and it really *is* terrible if we don't; we *must* have warmth, and we *will* die if we don't; we *must* have attention and it really *will* be the end of the world if we don't get it.

Now that we're adults, however, we can afford to be a little more flexible in our outlook. Being denied or rejected by our parents would have been fatal; being denied or rejected by our employer, spouse, colleague or friend is much less disastrous.

WHY ARE DEMANDS A PROBLEM?

The intensity of the demand is matched by the intensity of the disappointment and discomfort we anticipate if we don't get what we want. This, naturally, makes us rather driven and anxious about the outcome. We retreat back into our comfort zone, afraid to risk such damaging consequences even when the rewards of doing so are high.

The result is often a self-fulfilling prophecy. We put so much emotional investment into the result – we want it so badly and are so afraid of failing – that we fail to see the opportunities and take the calculated risks necessary to achieve it. We consequently often end up more uncomfortable, less satisfied and more anxious than if we had been less intensely demanding in the first place.

People who are natural positive thinkers take things much more lightly. They would *like* things to happen, they would *prefer* things to happen, they take vigorous action to ensure that what they want has an excellent chance of happening. But it wouldn't be an absolute, devastating catastrophe if it didn't. They don't have the same intense emotional attachment to a specific, inflexible outcome. Paradoxically, they are much more likely to get what they desire.

OVERCOMING DEMAND THINKING
Put things into perspective by following the examples of positive thinking in Part One:
- Learn to relax
- Adopt a broadminded attitude
- Be generous in your interpretation of events
- Realistically accept that life is less than perfect

You can also cultivate preferences in the place of demands.

Preferences are much more positive than demands. They are based on expectation, anticipation and enjoyment, whereas demands are based on fear, dread and anxiety. Preferences can be pursued with as much passion as demands. With less negative emotional attachment to the outcome, however, failure is much less threatening.

This means that you can risk being more flexible. You can set about getting preferences met much more easily, and with a much more open-minded and positive attitude, than you can with demands. You can be more creative and inventive about both the method and the results – less driven, blinkered and inflexible.

Take conscious action to turn your demands into preferences:
- Recognize when you are being driven by a demand
- Turn your demand into a preference

Recognizing demand thinking
There are usually clear signals that you are becoming intense and anxious about a want or desire:
- **Physical tension**
  Your nervous system becomes stimulated and you can't stay calm and relaxed about what you want. Your stomach tightens, you become tense just thinking about it.

- **Negative emotions**
  Rather than pleasure at the thought of what you want, you feel negative emotions such as anxiety, frustration, resentment, anger or fear at the thought of not achieving it or of losing it.
- **'Catastrophizing'**
  You imagine feeling terrible, or that terrible things will happen, if you don't get what you want.
- **Obsession**
  Your thoughts and feelings keep returning to the subject. You find it hard to let things take their course, or to get on with other tasks.

When you notice these warning signs, look for an underlying demand. Ask yourself what you feel *must* or *must not* happen, and what you fear the consequences to be.

Turning demands into preferences
The most effective way of changing demands into preferences is to consciously and persistently change the actual words we use when talking about what we want, need and expect.

Whether talking to other people or thinking about things to yourself, substitute 'preference' words for 'demand' words:

Example:

Demand words	Preference words
must	prefer
ought	like
should	can
have to	may
got to	hope

By using different words rigorously and consistently, you can consciously build up a more positive way of thinking, feeling and behaving.

When you catch yourself being driven by a demand or catastrophizing about an outcome, try replacing negative statements with positive ones.

Example:

Demand	Preference
My employer *must* treat me fairly, and if he doesn't that means he's a terrible person and I am a worthless one.	I would *prefer* my employer to treat me well, but if he doesn't I can assertively take steps to remedy the situation.
You *must* like me, and if you don't you're cruel, unfair and damaging.	I'd *prefer* you to like me, but if you don't I'll just spend more time with people who do.
My efforts *must* be rewarded amply, and if they aren't it's a great tragedy.	I'd *like* my efforts to be rewarded, but if they aren't, that's life. I've enjoyed myself anyway.

Try also to become aware of the way that demands can sabotage your goals and purpose:

Example:

Demand	Obstacle	Result
I *must* perform my job perfectly in all ways and at all times.	I make a mistake.	It's *terrible*, so I get stressed and become flustered; try to deny the mistake; fail to learn from it; avoid that area in future; perform badly.

Preference	Obstacle	Result
I *prefer* to perform well rather than badly.	I make a mistake.	It's *uncomfortable*, but I stay relaxed and look for ways to sort out the mistake; learn from it and become more competent in that area; perform better in future.

Things that help

It's not always easy to recognize demands for what they are and to remember to turn them into preferences. Two things that help are:

Relaxation

Follow the relaxation exercises in Chapter 3, *Energy*, to help relax the physical tension associated with demands. Being relaxed rather than stressed will help you to put things into a more positive perspective.

Visualization
While you are relaxed, imagine yourself behaving positively and effectively. Visualize enjoying putting your
preferences into effect, rather than being driven by
demands.

Recall a time when you found yourself reacting negatively
because of a demand. Now see yourself responding calmly
and rationally instead; what do you say, what do you do,
how do you feel?

Imagine yourself being much more relaxed about outcomes in the future. Imagine not getting what you want.
Rather than catastrophizing and telling yourself that it's
awful, terrible, unbearable, see yourself responding with a
shrug as you move on to the next thing. What do you say
to yourself, what do you do, how do you feel?

SUMMARY
Overcome demand thinking:
- Learn to recognize the 'symptoms' of a demand
- Replace demands with preferences
  - replace demanding words with more relaxing ones
  - replace negative, demanding statements with more
    positive ones
  - replace catastrophic outcomes with more realistic
    ones
- Recognize how demands actually sabotage your intentions

11

COMPARISONS

WHAT ARE COMPARISONS?

One thing that is almost certain to sabotage a positive approach to life is making comparisons, yet we do it all the time. We can find ourselves comparing:

- ourselves to others
- ourselves to an ideal
- our present lives to the lives of others
- our present lives to a fantasy ideal or a golden past

While there is value in encouraging the best from ourselves, and in living up to our own standards, there is little to be gained from trying to see how well or badly we do in comparison to other people.

Hearing that someone has achieved promotion in a job that holds no interest for us, mastered a skill that has no appeal for us, or attained a position at odds with our values, shouldn't cause us to negatively question our own performance. But sometimes it does, especially when our self-esteem is at a low ebb.

WHY DO WE COMPARE OURSELVES?

We have a natural curiosity, and a tendency to see how we measure up to others. When we are young, this helps us to develop – to find our place in the community, and to appreciate the stages we will ourselves achieve during growing up.

This natural tendency to find out where we fit in can easily develop into competition however, and is sometimes encouraged from an early age. As we get older we're ranked against each other in exams and sports, and often actively encouraged to become competitive. While not intrinsically bad, comparisons like these can take on a negative edge when there are rewards and punishments for success or failure. Our own performance becomes of less value than our performance compared to others.

It's not surprising that, as adults, we find ourselves comparing our attainments, our lifestyle, even our values and commitments to those of others. It's also of little surprise that we feel anxious if we perceive a failure to measure up to others.

WHY ARE COMPARISONS A PROBLEM?
Competition and comparison focus our attention on what others are doing and how they are performing, rather than focusing it on what we want to do.

They distract us from our purpose in life. They also lead to unnecessary, unhelpful questions about what we *should* be doing (in comparison to everyone else) or what we *ought* to be doing (in comparison to everyone else). We might also start worrying about what other people think of our values and purpose in life. Will they approve of them and think them worthwhile?

Constant comparison can make us question our intentions, undermine our sense of purpose and motivation, and cause negative states such as:
• jealousy
• anxiety
• egotism
• shame
• hopelessness
• uncertainty
• anger
• defeat

At its extreme, persistent comparison with others can lead to:
• conformity
• passivity

- lack of identity
- perceived inferiority
- insecurity
- possessiveness
- hostile competitiveness

Naturally positive people have a strong tendency to measure themselves only against their own standards and not against other people. They are firmly grounded in themselves and, while they admire and respect the achievements of others, they rarely feel that they have to compete with them.

Interestingly, some of the happiest, healthiest, most positive people have been found to be those who could be called natural eccentrics. Although they may take things to extremes, they have a very strong sense of purpose based exclusively on their own values, and pay very little attention, if any, to what anyone else thinks of them. This makes them very secure in themselves and encourages an optimistic, positive approach to life.

OVERCOMING COMPARISONS

Adopt the positive attitudes outlined in Part One:
- Understand what your own individual values, roles and purpose in life are
- Set your own goals and plan your own actions
- Focus on your successes and appreciate that they are due to your own individual talent and hard work
- Understand what motivates you, and what you find rewarding

In addition to the above, cultivate individuality and independence:
- Become consciously aware of when, where and how you compare yourself with others, or find yourself competing with them
- Develop your own ideas, thoughts, opinions and activities

- Recognize and accept that you have a right to your individual values, just as others have a right to theirs

Become aware of comparisons

When you find yourself making comparisons, stop. Focus instead on the positive things about yourself and your life.

Notice when you compare yourself to anyone else, or to some unrealizable ideal. Write it down – this record will help you to pick up any recurring themes or underlying patterns:

Example:

Monday	Visit H. Admire new flat and find myself wishing I lived in the city instead of the country. Uncertain that I've made the right move.
Tuesday	Read magazine. Admire thin models. Feel insecure and unattractive. Wonder if I should go on a diet.
Wednesday	D promoted. Remember that it could have been me if I'd stayed with J&J and feel jealous.
Thursday	See romantic film. Wonder why I don't have that sort of relationship and feel anxious and rejected.
Friday	Meet R. Feel slightly superior because baby means she can't work and is financially dependent on T.

Next, write a rebuttal to the comparison, focusing on positive things and, where possible, recalling your values:

Example:

Monday	Visit H. Admire new flat and find myself wishing I lived in the city instead of the country. Uncertain that I've made the . right move.	Recall original reasons for move: more space, better air, good for walks, more peaceful. In keeping with my value of a simple, healthy life (rather than a glamorous one!).
Tuesday	Read magazine. Admire thin models. Feel insecure and unattractive. Wonder if I should go on a diet.	I already eat a good, nourishing diet. Feel and look healthy and energetic because of it.
Wednesday	D promoted. Remember that it could have been me if I'd stayed with J&J and feel jealous.	I left J&J to go freelance in line with my values of independence and creativity (I didn't want to be promoted into management).

| Thursday | See romantic film. Wonder why I don't have that sort of relationship and feel anxious and rejected. | It's fiction! *Nobody* has a relationship like that. Remember values of independence and equality. |
| Friday | Meet R. Feel slightly superior because baby means she can't work and is financially dependent on T. | Independence is one of my values, not R's. Her values are entirely different and just as good. She is doing what she wants to do, I am doing what I want to do. |

Doing this over a period of time should help you bring your attention back to yourself and your concerns rather than focusing negatively on comparisons with other people.

Develop your own ideas

Get to know yourself better. Reflecting on your values is an excellent way to do this. You can also put yourself in contact with yourself, remind yourself who you are and how you might have changed by considering the following questions.

Take time to think about them and actually write down the answers so you can look back over them later:

- The five words that describe me best are . . .
- The five things I most enjoy doing are . . .
- I currently feel strongly about . . .
- I have been most affected recently by . . .
- When I was little I wanted to be . . .
- Today I want to be . . .
- My childhood hero/ine was . . .
- My current hero/ine is . . .
- I am at my best . . .
- I am happy when . . .
- I am proudest of . . .
- I would give up everything for . . .
- I wouldn't give up . . . for anything
- I would like . . . to be recognized and appreciated
- If I could do what I wanted right now, I would . . .
- If I could do what I wanted next week, I would . . .
- If I could do what I wanted for the rest of my life, I would . . .

- The five things I think are most important are . . .
- . . . makes me feel hopeful
- . . . makes me laugh
- I always thought I would grow up to . . .
- I am most glad that I . . .

There are no right or wrong answers to these questions. They are simply there to focus your attention on what you think, feel and believe.

Recognizing and accepting
It helps to remember that everybody – yourself included – has certain basic rights. These can be useful if you feel a bit insecure or uncertain of your individuality. Recalling your rights can help you to feel clear about the value of having your own ideas and beliefs.

I have the right to
- make my own decisions
- decide what I want
- decide what I need
- decide what I like or don't like
- make my own mistakes
- have self-respect
- express my own feelings
- express my own opinions
- express my own values
- say yes or no as I decide appropriate
- ask for what I want
- change my mind
- (and so does every other human being on this planet)

Repeat them to yourself frequently. They allow you to appreciate the values and opinions of others while focusing your attention firmly on your own.

SUMMARY
Overcome comparisons:

- Become aware of when and where you tend to compare yourself with others or compete with them:
  - notice how you compare yourself
  - counter the comparison with a positive statement
- Get to know and appreciate your own ideas and opinions better
- Understand your rights

SUMMARY: BECOMING A POSITIVE THINKER

All of us were born with a capacity for positive thinking that served us well during early childhood. We acquired the habit of negative thinking as we grew up and experienced negative attitudes and discouragement from the world around us. Just as we learned to be pessimistic, so we can learn to regain our positivity and optimism by doing what natural positive thinkers do.

Becoming, and remaining, a positive thinker entails taking a positive attitude – to yourself, to other people and to the world around you. With that positive approach, you should soon see life opening up for you as you expand your potential and broaden your horizons.

If this book had to be summed up into three key things to remember for a positive life, they would be:

- **Focus on the positive**
  Look out for positive things – search out the positive aspects of situations and events. Spend time with positive people; encourage positive attitudes; look for opportunities to enjoy yourself and focus on pleasant things.

  Minimize the time you spend dwelling on negative things, and avoid as much as possible people and things that lower your energy and make you feel down.

- **Speak positively to yourself**
  Change the voice in your head from one that criticizes and complains into one that supports and encourages you.

  Concentrate on making positive statements to yourself about yourself, your behaviour, and about the world in general.

- **Act positively**

  You don't have to wait, pretend you already *are* a positive person – have a purpose in life, look for solutions, be supportive and encouraging to yourself and others.

  Hold your head up, put your shoulders back and smile. Look positive and you will feel positive. Give yourself positive feedback at every opportunity.